DIFFRACTIONS

By Peter Dale

POETRY

Edge to Edge
Local Habitation
One Another
Under the Breath

TRANSLATIONS

Dante: *The Divine Comedy*

Tristan Corbière: *Wry-Blue Loves*
Poems of Jules Laforgue
Poems of François Villon
Paul Valéry: *Charms*

INTERVIEWS

Peter Dale in Conversation with Cynthia Haven
Michael Hamburger in Conversation with Peter Dale
Richard Wilbur in Conversation with Peter Dale

Peter Dale

Diffractions

New and Collected Poems

ANVIL PRESS POETRY

Published in Great Britain in 2012
by Anvil Press Poetry Ltd
Neptune House 70 Royal Hill London SE10 8RF
www.anvilpresspoetry.com

This book is published with financial assistance
from Arts Council England

Designed and set in Monotype Ehrhardt by Anvil
Printed and bound in Great Britain
by Hobbs the Printers Ltd

ISBN 978 0 85646 439 3

A catalogue record for this book
is available from the British Library

DEDICATION

Poems, the emphasis, essence of my edgy existence,
threads that darn-well stitched up everything done or undone,
rhymed, imagist, cadenced, journeying in books of hours,
artistically, assiduously – acid-free – you issued the scattered leaves.

Acknowledgements

The sections entitled *Diffractions* and *Foursquare* are published in book form for the first time.

Poems in *Diffractions* and *Foursquare* have appeared in the following publications: *Acumen*; *Agenda*; *All Through Language*; *The Anglo-Welsh Review*; *The Big Little Poem Series*; *The Clarion*; *Core*; *Dream Catcher*; *The Formalist* (USA); *The Interpreter's House*; *The London Magazine*; *Mairi MacInnes: A Tribute*, ed. Peter Robinson; *Outposts*; *Poetry Salzburg Review* (Austria); *Proof*; *Quattrocento*; *The Rialto*; *Stand*; *The Swansea Review*; *The Use of English*. Forty epigrams from *Foursquare* were first published in *Eight by Five*, 2007, a limited edition by Rack Press.

'And There Was Light' and 'Orpheus in Darkness' were published in *Peter Dale in Conversation with Cynthia Haven*, BTL, 2005.

'Archival', 'For Aspen' and 'The Unknown Flower' first appeared in *Branch-Lines*, edited by Lucy Newlyn and Guy Cuthbertson, Enitharmon, 2007.

The author is grateful to the following publishers for permission to reprint epigrams from books they have published: The Hippopotamus Press, Agenda Editions and Rack Press.

Introduction: Hounds of Spring

ROBERT FROST speaks teasingly of taking the road less travelled by; his friend Edward Thomas took the road heavily travelled to the First World War trenches. Both led to remarkable poetry. The vocation of being a poet does not have an established path. There is no road through the wood – or dark forest.

The compulsion is a bloodhound called Obsession which drags you after a scent that has no detectable path. When young you think it is your hound but it is for some the hound of Heaven; for others a hell-hound; for many poets an alternation of the two. I hoped it was an earth-hound. (In my teen-age years, my first non-family reader was a dustman who picked up and read twelve lines of my verse blown from the dustbin and commented to my stepmother in the garden, ''Ere, this is good stuff.') Pasternak said that poetry 'will always be in the grass. You will need to bend down to hear it.'

So the books along this pursuit took their titles by reference to the classical elements of earth, air, fire and water, as does this volume.

In the modern world we rather overlook some of the vital silences of life: the silence of a sleeping child, that companionable silence of old friends, the silence of the death room. The silence of remembrance has been re-established nationally. Silences may be golden; silence can be cut with a knife when it collides with us as we enter a room where people have been discussing us. The uncanny silence before a storm affects more than humanity. The moments of silence at the tide's turning come like a surprise.

Religion and the arts are empowered by silence, both as a means and as an effect. As a child I used to feel intensely the silence before a service began. The silence in a concert hall after a great piece of music ends is palpable. Music and poetry employ silences for many of their effects.

Emily Dickinson remarked that the voice has only one inflection [at a time] but that the pen has many. You cannot make anyone's poem *work* for another reader by argument. You can only pass it to them to read, hoping that it speaks in the silence of the inner ear. Which brings us to Pasternak's 'power of deafening silence' and touches upon Wittgenstein's remark: 'whereof one cannot speak thereof one must be silent.' That, say, is the ideal poem.

Someone has said that producing a Collected Poems is like nailing down your own coffin lid – a curious advantage, perhaps, over other people – but an endeavour that fills one with trepidation. Given the waywardness of the earth-hound on the scent, selected volumes are attempts of poets at various stages in their careers, or careering after the hound, to level things to the standard of their best work. That is an understandable but forlorn hope because the mind is not a fixed point of judgement and the writer's preference towards the chosen poems may change after publication. Friends and readers, perhaps more detached than the author, will hasten to suggest mistaken inclusions and exclusions. The poet can only answer like Shaw's St Joan: with whose judgement may I judge except my own? – And hope the work's fate is not hers.

A *Collected Poems* may suggest that the poet feels the end of the tether slipping from the hound, as well may be – except that poets know the fickle springs of poetry but not where the spring line ends. Several have found miraculous late springs. A Collected may be no firmer than earlier selections were. The hope is that the rest is not silence.

This collection is an expansion of the selected poems, *Edge to Edge*. The text of that is left virtually unaltered, though one or two poems previously overlooked have been included. It also contains the bulk of the volumes published since *Edge to Edge*, long out of print. The title-selection, *Diffractions*, is new as is the selection of epigrams, *Foursquare*. The narrative sequence, *Local Habitation*, still available, has been left for a later volume. There is half a century of experience and poems here, a few first published in *Walk from the House*, 1962.

Contents

1 DIFFRACTIONS

from HAVING NO ALTERNATIVE

THE GOING

3 *from* UNDER THE BREATH (2002)

I

Diffractions

I saw it as my task to revive the idea of poetry, printed in books, on pages which speak with the power of deafening silence.

BORIS PASTERNAK

reported in *Meetings with Pasternak* by Alexander Gladkov, translated by Max Hayward

In Memoriam

Pat Strouvelle (1916–2007)

Wisteria

If we were superstitious we'd not be surprised,
you garden lover, how the thirty-yard wisteria
we photographed you under on your ninetieth
withered a year later the week you died.
You had no truck with anything mysterious
and least of all the rigmaroles of death.
Well, now, green-fingers, if anyone can,
you can, wherever you happen to be:
we wouldn't be surprised next year to see
the thirty yards of wisteria bloom again.

Child's Play

Home Visit

Warmed in the hand, almost bone,
nostalgia, I cannot clench more
into the wet chill of this stone,

and lob it out into the bourn,
identified a moment before
merging among the water-worn,

and in the gravels lost to sight.
A child will find it moist one day
to cool a summer, grasp it tight.

Wingless bird, he'll fling it high,
its impress gone, and time to play.
Fly away, Peter, hit the sky.

Second childhood.

Kids' Game

That whizz of a kids' game,
tag on the lines, joins, cracks
in the road's concrete slabs:

to foot-tag the shadow
of runners on those lines,
lank shanks in the low light.

One summer time.
But still the names come back
to the last man.

Catch as catch can
and close on one of the missed
to sign off on this.

Mike Baker

Jigsaw

Fiddling with that kid's desk of yours,
years after you have grown and gone,
idly I pulled out all the drawers.
There, in the 'secret' one, bits shone.

Clippings. Jigsaw of face on face,
cut from dozens of family snaps,
left in your pretend hiding-place.
None of the photos with the gaps.

No telling now if you'd concealed
the trusted or distrusted smiles,
nor if you wanted these revealed
once you were years away and miles.

We tried to give you a future, child,
but you have changed our past.
What love cut out, what hate reviled –
I hope you have what you recast.

Christening

Tide's out. My dam of sand right up the beach.
Stay up, hold back my reservoir of sea.
Quick, that crack, more sand.

It mustn't break. I mustn't see it break.
It mustn't, mustn't. The waves are sneaking back.
Mother, mother, call me in.

– That low voice of yours, uttering my name,
quietly in the dawn, as if for the first time,
how shall I escape it?

Through that door, that door never to close,
with the last call answering the echo?
Tears that run inward like time.

– Mother, do not appear to me now:
your birth-pangs were so long ago – your early death
more than your lifespan back.

Mother, do not come now, myself near ghost.
Late, it's too late. Time cannot be reversed.
The guilt is spent, has spent my life.

Eight years you left me to his tentacles,
the spineless grasp of ectoplasmic occlusion,
before he married up with earth.

Free? Free? Is that what you'd have said?
Set free, of both of you, dead free,
and let to go my own way?

Like that featureless heath? Find my own way.
Own way? I'll own-way you, my lad. Just you watch.
You'll see. – Hear, hear.

You call me by my name for the last time,
you disembodied voice, old woe-betide-you,
echo back to echo.

The door is shut. Don't try appearing now,
mum as a mist, miasma, willa the wisp.
Now there's a name for you.

The rock, the hollow rock, is answering back.
You never talked to me. How shall I speak?
Well, hear this. Hear this:

Only the word 'love' can be withdrawn.
Mother of dust, you cannot walk through walls.
How do you speak to your son?

I am dead to my son in my ghost flesh.
What have you done with my name? – Hush, now, hush.
– You brought me back rock.

I want to go out now: friends wait for me,
dead friends. I have too many dead to wear.
You'll have to go. 'Bye, byes.

Vignette

Some fifty years ago when you were left,
earth on the windswept hill of grubby sheep.
I'm nearly last of those who knew you lived –
stone dead before more love than need took shape.

You, sitting on the beach in a headscarf.
Me, out of earshot, faking the fun of sand.
– No football now and make sure not to scuff. –
Eye on the tide, longing for the day's end.

Sand-grains' discroaching, terrifying stealth,
wiggling down the castle, quick as newts.
If we had loved or hated at full tilt
the mind's eye might have taken more vignettes.

Your age at death a child's to my worn years,
my long-shots missed the mind behind your face.
Not much is left to go. Something of yours:
odd genes that jolt me into anger fast?

Is anger in the genes, then, and not love?
Love we must find over the wilds of years?
All those we never had: times that would leave
sheltered hollows, no void like yours and mine.

To Aspen

FOR JULIA AND HAMISH

They say life is the thing,
though grey, I prefer books.
I hope the luck will bring
those natural good looks
that you, considering
the mirror's glance, would choose
yourself; behind them, brains
that render books not pains
but pleasures to use.

Your father and my friend,
your mother and his wife,
with absolute love will tend
your being throughout life.
There is no need to send
one wish upon that score.
I hope that you respond
with love, a bungee bond
not felt a chore.

I wish the three of you
this gift safe as the breeze
the aspen whispers to
more softly than other trees:
I wish your parents true
pleasure in all the courses
of your work and leisure;
wish you that shared pleasure.
Though life, in Morse, is . . .

Harangues

Birthday List

A woman speaks

Gifts are a bridgeless river;
    true gifts contain the will
and spirit of the giver.
        Such gifts can spill.

Give me the holes in a sieve.
    I could take that from you.
What do you want to give?
        What's it to do?

Is it that bourn again,
    Death? I should like that.
Addressed with fancy pen,
        gift-wrapped, words pat.

It would have to be comfortable,
    to fit me like a glove.
It would be so beautiful,
        ideal, love.

But it must set me free
    of those who've died before.
I'd shut my eyes to see.
        Kid me once more.

Well, open your velvet glove.
    It must be precious little;
no hurt for those I love;
        noncommittal.

The dead should be free of our guilt,
    and they demand more dead
to rest under their earth-quilt
        – unparroted.

But tell me before I go
    to lie beneath some sod –
not that I need to know –
        how long you'll play god.

Then and Now

A woman speaks

I *Give and Take*

If you gave me a gift
I'd have to accept,
churlish to reject.
Pushy if you persist
without some clue
I'd acquiesce.
But you'd presume.

Some trinket I should like?
Most give what they want
or else some freebie con.
Showy but out of sight?
Something I lack?
How should I respond?
You would want thanks.

Would it be any use
or stuck on display?
(Do you know my tastes?)

Would it show off you?
So should it stand
in pride of place?
Should it be tit for tat?

Would you celebrate now
or commemorate
some auspicious day?
In some far cold house
is it to reminisce
some vanished grace?
That sort of thing?

What a song and dance
to make of a gift.
Sorry. Isn't it this,
the striptease arts,
you'd want to coax?
If some precious thing
these drawers will stow it.

Is it tastefully wrapped
with labels and love?
It's hardly enough.
What a gift-horse that.
I know what I want.
You never guess much.
Is peace in the offer?

Know how to box that?
And I'd want guarantees;
an instant end; no scenes;
and no heavenly act;
everything must go;
a closing sale – complete.
Don't give me a stone.

2 *Exit Speech*

And if I have been
as an ill friend to
you in this house
it is because
you have not found
my husband's love
worth the attempt –
whom in this death
I cannot bed.

Now I am going,
I thank you somewhat,
for that has been
kindly to me,
although my husband
would neither betray
me nor himself.
Now that I go,
I will not let go.

He has been kind,
oh, kind to me,
but he has no love
left for this wraith.
Here, take this ring,
and with this spell
it binds you both
into your selves
until it breaks.

The two of you
have failed me in this.
And, on my life,
gently you gave
all that I need,

not what I want.
You shall not touch
upon this ring
while ye both shall live.

This malice I speak
you have kindly given.
I return the gift
because you both
have refused the guilt
by which alone
a poor ghost is
to be recalled
from a cold grave.

Some Keepsake

I liked you, not your tricks.
And now you've tried this dodge.
No joke. It sticks
in the throat like stodge.

I do not want your desk,
firewood or heirloom.
The thing's grotesque.
I haven't the room,

the taste, or gratitude.
I used to think of you
in my time and mood,
without this cue.

This is the dust sheet
I've cobbled up on it,
with the odd beat
of a mad fit.

How could you try out death
permanently to worm
into my living breath
for the long term?

Second Comeback

FOR MILL STONE

Lethean, if you return
you'll have no memory
but I shall.
'To whom it may concern'
– that how you'll home on me?
Oh, salutations.

Who am I? You'd get it wrong,
your own identity
wiped to all-hallows.
But I remember scar-long
what you have been to me
behind face value.

You loved all that I was?
– Wanted it vacuum-packed,
immalleable,
stamped with a rugged cross.
Your last gasp failed in the act.
So valedictions:

Lethean, you can't return.
Your memory has gone.
Here goes the malice.
How in hell did you learn
love as that glutinous con
callous as hatred?

Retrospection

Retrospective: A Painter Speaks

FOR PHILIP HOY

Did you? I did. Imagine the life we'd have,
and while you lived there was still hope,
though now I scavenge through the screwn-up years
in our spoil heap:

the schemes, shared viewpoints, venues met or missed,
and rearrange them as ventures, fixtures,
to distance the memories that spite – appal.
Past beyond facts.

Pusillanimous palliatives. – All I can do
to mourn you more than the years lost,
spectral nuance. The past is what we make it,
old formalist.

This oil: the stand of willows centring the hayfield,
green waterfall short of a precipice –
I was there and don't say you never were.
I am and it is.

And that diminutive figure in the background,
is you, turned with your lost profile,
along the track, seeing up the hillside
that eyeful of dark yews.

Constitutional

Stage-whispering,
just a few yards ahead,
the fallen leaves
jostle, crowding towards us
like the souls of all our dead
in greedy welcome.

Orpheus in Darkness

FOR ROLAND JOHN

Where have you gone, Eurydice, oh, my love
of life? Where have you fled? In the dark,
the music casts no light; my hands lie dumb.
The pipes are broken and cracked the harp.
Eurydice, what music can be strung
on dry sticks? I'll find my voice. I'll bring you,
wherever you are held, a song of love.
It will marmorealize all Dis
to set you free. Orpheus, the singer,
swears you this.

Restaurant

Late, always late. If she'd show up . . . No joy.
But then in you mooch, the same old duffel coat.
No, your spit image it was – and such a jolt.
Never believed in ghosts, quiet or unquiet.

Anyway, thanks to his spooking turn and pause,
he'd raised your old wry grin, the doubtful glances,
our black-list updates of limelight worshippers.
Years since the last of our yarning liquid lunches.
I'm chronic years older than you'd be now,
twin sceptic, verging on the garrulous bore.
You'd not mistake this wreck for me, you know.
You'd miss me face to face, crossing the bar.
– Where is she? – Well, you'd said, nearing your exit,
boredom's more interesting the older you get.

Second Reading

IN MEMORIAM WILLIAM COOKSON

Time travel. Our favourite defunctive bard
that neither, years ago, thought worth a light –
where we agreed so well. Good for a laugh.

I'm thereabouts again so late in life,
since months ago you happened to remark
how recently you'd warmed to the odd line.

– Still clear, our jokes, the barred and gemlike flam.
I trudge between, in hopes of coming by
the lines you'd found, to share and understand.

It's even harder going now you're dead.
Our jokes, the fustian clag, and in three minds:
two dead and one still crawling to The End.

Just one more chance, old friend, to meet on words,
the last together, nailing lines of verse.

Way Out

IN MEMORIAM EDDIE WOLFRAM

My old mucker in the arts,
we'd thought these visits were the old
friendship for life on both our parts,
unchangeable – nothing untold.

But we were seeing the future come
where each must go in single file.
Your right hand and its cunning numb.
How shall we rig this loss of style?

The words are falling from me, friend.
Never was nifty with my hands.
Most things broken in the end.
How do we cross these quaking sands?

My shadow, your spread dead weight.

New Year Resolution

And that page might just as well go.
That too. Dates fast, an address book.
My turn to double-cross *that* crook.
Here goes, hatching his bungalow.

A splinter under the nail, your name
still hurts, lost friend. . . . Another pair
that split, and who knows which went where?
This bastard – vanished with his fame.

More dead . . . my old mucker. Dear friend,
without you I can hardly stay.
So many paths that led away.
So many things returned to sender.

More white ink cannot cope with it.
The paper-clipped step out of line;
pages inserted split the spine.
The book can never be rewritten.

Young strays to Zed. – Still, room to write
that kid's address, a second stray:
The Universe, The Milky Way,
The Solar System, Third Satellite,

The Earth, The Occident, Euroland,
Great Britain, Wales, Cardiff, This Street,
This house, This room. This pen – white sheet,
this shaky hand.

Aftertones

Epitaph: The War Graves

These stones no one shall roll away.
Nothing will bring an Easter day.
These men, forever sacrificed,
gave more than any risen Christ.

Seconding Harry Patch, Henry Allingham and the Fallen

Remembrance Day, the Cenotaph,
the wreaths, the regimented ranks,
it's show-business on death's behalf.
The dead would not, if they could, say thanks.

Archival

Another house beside a brook,
a similar beside a lane;
light-scribbled water, furrow line
of leaves beside the path, flint, brick.

So many snaps, such varied groups,
posh-tinted, sepia, black and white;
walls warm with sun or glinting wet:
street parties, weddings, birthdays, trips.

Family faces in unrelated hats,
extraordinary millinery finely poised;
subversive kids not to be posed,
cloth caps, trilbies on rigid heads.

Some named on margins or the back,
most nameless, taken by a love
that needed no reminders of
what was as known as heartbeat or break.

Smiles, in uneasy swimsuits, girls
all waving at the hidden eye.
Beyond, in glide-and-sideslip air,
the forlorn cries of silent gulls.

Bunting and kids' flag-wagging grins.
Behind, the absent ghost of a son
locked in the eye that framed the scene
where parents gaze back past the lens.

Not Brueghels, not Vermeers, anon.
One face, which face? the love of a life.
Light silvered on a wind-turned leaf.
The focus of the eye unknown.

The Unknown Flower

FOR E. T.

More yours than mine this countryside,
the high-ridged backbone to the day.
I keep an eye out all the way,
knowing you took it in your stride.

One, spirit of a time-torn house,
the other, of an ancient earth,
how should we meet by track or hearth
unless the house were ruinous?

Gusts in the broken panes. . . . Laid ghost,
though Arras, Agny mark your end,
haunt this high ridge where you are mourned.
– Betony, was that, or wishful guess?

My eye, unlike yours, not so sharp,
but, sharing your soft spot for rain,
I shelter in this leaky ruin,
trying to fix leaf, colour, shape.

Your stateliest of small flowers?
No whisper. Whatever plant it is,
today has made it in my eyes
another flower that was yours.

'Markway steeplet', its pseudonym:
spectator of the passing spectres,
high above the hectared acres;
this way we meet within a name.

The Dead

1939–1945

This copse the place – two butterflies that mime
quick fingers flickering out a plait of light.
Lest we forget – as I would, that lampless time –
whenever here I'll try to think on you,
your service to this land. . . . In winter, too,
when bare trees jag black lightning at the sight.

The hands of all the tortured dead that stir
in supplication for their leaves again.
Oh spring-fresh willow-green, oh Lincoln green.
And no more chosen than your parents were,
under the *diktat* of your death and pain,
than stone-cold names of heroes you'd not been.

Tidying Up

The baggy army beret, the face.
Bernard's, my sister's brother-in-law,
seen in my school-days once at her place;
soon after dead, some flaw in the heart.

An armoured car in the photograph,
and, from all this sand, a Desert Rat –
half-smiling, but more skew-faced the laugh
that my recollection latches on.

Oh, your face, Keith Douglas, your smile
that jolts me back with this photo-fit

of memory's outcast, slipped from a file.
Yet I know only your written words.

Bernard, long dead, unwalking ghost,
I think I have remembered you.
Dead or alive, not much to boast.
What are you to do with these words?

Making Peace

The desert's unforgiving.
        The last time they came
                they bulldozed its dust
over the living.
        They set the torrid air aflame
                and said the war was just.

The long arm of their law,
        they thought they were
                the world's police.
Quick on the draw,
        they never heard
                Ozymandias keep the peace.

And There Was Light

IN MEMORIAM R. V. DALE (1932–2003)

Sun through the autumn pear-trees,
leaves a translucent flock of ambers
like benign fire.

The beauty is not in the air,
not in the leaves, not in the lambency
but in the mind's eye

that is dying – stark staring.
Not enough, the spectral ambience.
What was it, light?

Eyes that have seen you fare
lampless into the curtained blackout.
Brother, our long good bye.

Maybe Words for Music

Heugh

FOR W. S. MILNE

Ma luve it greits as deep an narra
as cleaves the Linn o Dee
whase skiran cletters in ma marra
as na mair sall she.

Her bed is narra, na sae deep,
the kirk athoot ae tree,
an there sae douce an saft her sleep
she dreams na mair o me.

Wheesht, wheesht tha stushie, fa,
whilk blethers in ma lug.
I canna heark her laich laich ca –
her sough wadna lift a speug.

Wheesht, wheesht tha haivers, fa.
Tha slitteran in ma banes
Canna mak ma sarra sma
as tha may mirl thae stanes.

Song

Now go away. Just go away.
You've kept this up a year.
High time to sling your hook. What's here?
A clinging clay.

I left you life and not this black.
Now leave the rest to me.
The leaves are down from the dead tree.
That's the path back.

Let snowdrops, crocus, daffodils
still calendar your days.
Head for the trill of the heat haze
and sun-shot stills.

And don't come back. Neither alone
nor hand in hand, my dear,
for if you do, cold as this stone,
one will stay here.

The earth is jealous of the living;
they're jealous of the earth.
And both of them are unforgiving
of death, love, birth.

Blade

Well, you can have your paradise
if that is what you want.
Go, high above the poor church mice
and name-worn font,

but let me tell you this, dear sprite:
if, on some timeless day,
minding your groundless state of light,
on your boundless way,

you find one blade of real grass pokes
        between two airless thoughts,
you'll yearn for fields of grass and oaks,
                shade of all sorts;

and so you'll take and lay that blade
        between your ideal thumbs,
wanting the reedy note once played,
                but no sound comes,

because that blade grew from my grave
        and I shall be in it,
rooted in earth, nor further crave
                some vapid flit.

Envoy: To P.

There is no life without you.
But the words, these words,
they shall never leave you;
they will remain speaking
even in long silence,
like glances given in secret
between consensual couples
divided by company.

2

From

Edge to Edge

(1996)

From *The Storms*

Dedication

Here, Ian, a few poems, a decade's debris,
made and emended in odd moments.
Lines I like first to leave with you
only, my friend. Now free to all.

The Storms

Losing my patience, setting type in the press
you gave me, I can hear your voice insist
Paul was no artist since he would untwist
knots you'd snip and slash. Such pithiness
from you, thought worthy once to break a spell
of silence, startles me and I recall
how far away you are, crowding with all
your work into a room in Camberwell.

Once, as I walked with your usual silent self,
you spoke out: A bag of peanuts equals the weight
of Boehme's works; your pockets bulged with great
wisdom but meagre food. Here, on the shelf,
your Boehme lies. Thumbprints of paint edge
your favourite lines. They mark my books you read,
snatched in frenzy to back something you said,
or rammed beneath your easel as a wedge.

Outside the study window now the tree
I tried describing, you to draw, is a flare
of shuffling leaves. All that's left of the bare
boughs are my words and these two or three
sketches recalling how your hands would form
a winter-struck tree whenever you discussed
the way you start a carving. . . . A slight gust
rustles the leaves but ushers in no storm.

Rainbow's trajectory zooms over the scarp
shoulder plunging right into the town
huddled beneath the shelter of the down.
And I think of other trajectories: your sharp

erratic course through towns; sketches that lie
discarded in lodgings like a paper trail
no one can track; this tree you traced as a frail
skeletal hand to close against the sky.

The leaves will motley soon, ready to drop.
The first winds will flail the branches bare.
I set alight the sketches I kept; they flare,
darken and gnarl. . . . You could come and stop
the winter. Then perhaps your hands would rouse
to shape this tree again. The slate light
wouldn't disturb your photophobic sight.
Come and bring your storm into my house.

The window casts a broken shaft of light
towards the darkness. The valley lights wink out,
one at a time. Your tree rustles about
my shadowed head. This lamp is seen for quite
a distance. But not by you. Nothing can find
you in that darkness where your sketches sail
like papers from a house ransacked by gale.
Come back, for the storm beats into my mind.

I stare my face out, glad that some have sworn
we're brothers. But your nose is longer; your lips
curve with the sensuous line of women's hips –
mine are a scar. And brothers, we know, are born
of one woman's suffering. . . . Yet we have led
a wandering life together, and I've known
your hands gnarl into a tree of bone.
And, tonight, your storm beats into my head.

Last light vanishes. . . . Cold night air creeps
under the doors and windows, up my back.
Wind begins to rush and with a crack
the branches sway. A single leaf sweeps

against the pane, a moth the glass deceives.
Rain beats like canvas tearing. I draw
the blinds across the distorted face I saw.
Take shelter. Late birds bicker in the eaves.

Overnight Coach

Shot with sleep, the head slumps on the chest.
Ribs jolt against me every corner swing.

But I don't know your name or anything,
though my shoulder would afford some kind of rest.

I sit in arm's reach to cushion your back
but you have to lean against a travel bag.

And yet I stay awake in case you sag,
for then my hand could save your head a crack.

The flail of speeding branches claws great rents
across your face, projected as if dead.

And if I cannot shoulder your sleeping head
it is because time comes I may not raise

your bowed head from its tears. The road strays
briefly through England. And there are continents.

Eighth Period

Last year's sex-kitten, out of work again,
(mean effrontress, chased and bare)
saunters about the grounds with her great Dane,
as sandy blonde as that lassitude of hair –
boy-hunting, leash seductively in hand.
Four o'clock and time to make a stand.

I plot my progress through the room to reach
the window for a glimpse of her, compare
her insinuity with these hulks I teach,
mobile jumble-sales with sweep's-brush hair.
One week to go. Difficult to think
by then they'll learn to dress like her and slink.

Drama for Today. She reads a speech,
a mother deprived of husband and only son
in the World War. (Once more undo her breach,
dear friends.) The long day's task is done.
The slumping class as usual does not hear,
luckily. She speaks with passion. And they'd jeer.

Only I hear and follow closely now,
head in the book to hide my smarting eyes,
tensing for fear I have to pick a row
with some lout there before that passion dies.
This part of her may last until the bell,
perhaps a year. A glance outside may tell.

Untrammelled sunset across the silt plain
leans in the window, deriding all shapes,
knocking the shadows sideways once again.
Chalk dust solidifies two broken scapes
propped on the sill. Some day soon
that girl will find her shadow squat at noon.

And this one? She'll leave, now that she can,
to work for drinks, good lays and a night's rest.
And then she'll feel it in her bones how man
is easy straight up or flat out at best;
till at her gate one evening she will stand
watching his shadow deformed by ploughed land.

Single Ticket

The train rattles through the night.
That face opposite: more sallow now,
yet still that hair mists into light,
the skin more mobile on the brow.
A lapse of memory . . . or time.
Gone that sidelong
glance her eyes had, green as lime.
Caught in scrutiny of a face,
they lowered like a dog's in disgrace.
Now tears rim those eyes once strong.

Time and again she glances my way.
Unsure, I wonder whether she tries
to place me or return the stray
stares I prolong to recognize
her features. I turn to the dusty pane,
and there's her face,
wrinkled and weeping in the driving rain.
Illness or time might make her look
like this. I nod back to my book,
returning through years to the old place.

A trick of memory, commonsense
insists. There's a ring on her hand.
Too much depends on coincidence
for one homecoming in years to land
me on this branch of the local line
in the same train
with her, however changed those fine
features, the laughter corded round
the lips. I stare again as if bound
to catch some trait clinchingly plain.

That battered case offers no clue,
no name, no label. Travelling alone,
she troubles me like one I knew
by sight those years ago, the tone
of her voice unheard. I do not speak
and nor does she.
If once we'd broken week after week
of this we might have joined the train
together, and her eyes not show such pain.
I doubt it, though. She stares at me.

My stop. She gets out further down
the corridor and runs as once she ran,
when late, to catch her train to town –
or any woman runs to dodge a man
who eyes her too intently. I walk
the other way,
and two miles home, rehearsing talk
to come. Her heels tick into night.
– More faces to reshape at sight,
their recognitions to outstare next day.

Not Drinking-Water

Home after years, tonight,
cleaning my teeth,
I taste the waters of childhood,
still unfluoridated,
tangless, not tepid, quite –
once an apple-slicing chill
by which all quenchings could be placed.

Suddenly minute fear,
not noticing the granary tower
by the old mill pond
that used to dominate the sky round here.
– Dwarfed
a little beyond
some concrete block for storing flour.

The water I've tasted:
shower, river, full of lime,
brine of the eyes,
sweat of her brow,
hard and soft and somewhere sour.
This taste I seem to forget.
I have been thirsty all my life.

Last Respects

I know these hands, their feel,
knew of the cuts beneath the scars
and wondered when the split nail would heal.

They used to lark
with birds of shadow on the wall
for children scared of the dark.

Fall now –
and all the birds are flown.

Hunched shadows black the wall.

Meditation down the Wards

I look for some characteristic in each face
that marks them out for pain and sacrifice,
but they are all so different, some like myself,
so that I pass white-coated but unsafe.

Because there's so much agony to life
I would erect suffering into a belief,
make these men its martyrs and its saints,
and marvel at their useless innocence.

But just to state, though true, their pain is real
seems traitor, and to found on pain some rule
and order, callous. I'm a coward if I daren't
insist their pain's a pointless accident.

These faces do not change. They all are marked
by pictograms of grief, and they are mocked
by this pseudo-smile I try, in fear and guilt,
to some response, though faked and difficult.

Patient in a Ward

He holds his hand out like a sunflower drooping,
palm foremost on stalk wrist, the fingers
undone in dead petals hooking backward.

But this is no paper flower held waiting
in charity upon the street corners
to pass by with twopence or blank eyes lowered.

He is in pain. It is death thrusting
his hand out. – The desperation falters
seeing me reach for words of comfort.

The Visitors

They know no more than I would how to stand
with flowers, and, being men, sheepishly clutch
them, elbows stiffly bent,
as though a touch
of clothes or hand
would wither up the bloom and kill the scent.
They do not know the odd resilience of flowers.
They wait for wife's or child's visiting hours.

Shot on jets of green the tulips zoom
and weigh their stems across the corridors,
heavy and symmetric as eggs.
The visitors
need so much room
the trolleys brush the flowers or knock their legs.

They hinder the stretcher bearing one whose life
hangs in the balance. Someone else's wife.

Then for a nurse they thin to single file
and let her through to supper as though she rushed
to tend an injury.
Awkward and hushed,
they try a smile,
then shift and fidget, stood without dignity
at the beck and call of junior nurse or maid,
shielding their flowers, helpless, almost afraid.

Just Visiting

And you are one of these faces. At first
unseen, then recognized right down the ward.
A twitch of greeting since I couldn't wear
as far as that a smiling face, held fast.

You whine how much your cut hurts. You tell
me nurses forced you up to pack their wads
for sterilizing, made you decorate the ward's
long walls with flowers. And you quite ill.

I'm supposed to be horrified, to sympathize.
Yet nurses have to get the dressings done,
Nightly have boys to lay and drinks to down,
like you, to make their leaving home worth this:

Sister's periods, the old and wrinkled faces
pursed on nerve-strings to the clenched lips,
hours of obedience enough to bring collapse
on hangover, and, then, cleaning up faeces.

And some of them have indolent golden hair.
Over there, a woman is dying, the line
of used laughter hung in bands on the lean
bones. . . . And what you say I cannot hear.

I shudder. If your eyes started to glaze
I should listen now, although it could not lead
again to lively talk, drinks, light to slide
about your belly like brandy in a glass.

Such compassion couldn't save a hair,
not give a breather. . . . But you will live again,
and the living need a little love to go on.
You can speak now. I am here.

Obtainable from all good Herbalists'

The eyes of your trinket laughter
are with me, they dance in the street,
like moon-skittering water;
I can hardly walk straight.

Oh, what shall I do
with all these lights on route?
They will not distil a dew
to necklace your bright throat.

Hesitant, I halt
outside the herbalist's
for purslane and burdock held
to lengthen our lives and lusts.

Half-humorously I scan
the galleonate window bay:
julep, moly to gloss the skin.
Almost I enter and buy.

Yet if I bought a phial,
some glassblower's masterpiece,
your health and joy to taste and feel,
that, after, as a vase would pass –

A careless wave of ease,
twin crescents of your laughter,
you'd flaunt before my face,
and then you'd drink plain water.

Sleek one, cultivate cats
with latex tongue and suede nose
for their flattering slinky coats.
Witch, you've taken my wits with your knees.

from THE MONTHS

Thrush

Dawn-light hatches her cheeks with shadow lashes.
Thinking I'm still asleep
she draws my fist to feel how well
her flesh is hummocked with child.
I let her, playing fast asleep,
and don't unclench my hand.
She claws my fingers over her bared stomach.
They feel a bird,
as though caught in the hand,
tremble and flinch.

Gazing out of the window above my desk
I start
as something plummets from the eaves,
close to the glass in the dusk.
A tile, I think,
tensed for the thud as it dives.

But a thrush mounts up in flight,
beats down the garden,
banks to miss the trees, and greys
into night without trace.

Still tense for the thud,
I sit till quite late.

Riverside Garden

She sits drinking tea
in the river-garden,
a wing of hair
folded over her small ear.

Three packets of biscuits
she insisted on
tumbled like children's bricks
on the table here.

A Brutalist tower of glass
rockets from shrubs behind her,
a skinny silver birch
shading her shoulders.

Across the table
a spring-heeled sparrow
bounces
in its search.

She breaks a biscuit
to draw them all around.
One of the packs
already crumbles away.

She tries to aim the crumbs
to cheat the pigeons;
more sparrows gather
and clutter up the tray.

Another pack gone.
Now for the last.
– Ornithosis. Bird-shit.
Germ-ridden claws.

Useless to speak or say
birds shouldn't feed on crumbs,
Pregnant or not,
a lost cause.

Matchstick city clerks
stride to their trains
important
in their hurry home.

They glare in passing
at two provincials
who feed a pest of pigeons
and block the thoroughfare.

Bats

Eight months gone,
obsessed with birds,
at dusk she calls me to the window bay
to glimpse the fledglings trying out their wings
in grotesque flight
in our room
reflected by the lamps.

But they are bats.
Though, since her mind is turned to omens
and the oldwives' tales she's heard,
I do not speak.
The cry of bats is tuned beyond our hearing
but a child's is not so hard.

From *Mortal Fire*

Dedication

TO PAULINE

Your presence, love,
like the under-light
of trees within a wood,
that quiet pleasure
I could always predict,
often request.

But to tell you,
somehow share
this pleasure in writing,
always unbidden,
seldom predicted,
and solitary.

This you request of me
and I in return
promise to share
these ten years past,
yet find no words,
none like your presence.

Walk from the House

I chanced to tread on a stag-beetle on the walk
from the house. It creaked like wickerwork.

But when you, father, fell and came to die
no detonation wrecked the streets that day.

A great matter went out of the universe
and nothing shook beneath its radiant force.

It should have knocked a world to stellar dust
but only a day or two my hands were dazed.

Yet now I watch my step in a distant town
as though a mine were buried at each turn.

Unaddressed Letter

I had no need to come to your funeral.
I heard the news only by telegraph.
The shock I felt was distant and unreal.
Nor was there with me one so aged with grief
to need an escort to the open grave.
A letter could have made my peace instead.
I had no need to come, yet there I stood.

Sheep on the hill like huge maggots. 'God shall wipe
away all tears from their eyes
and there shall be no more death to weep;
neither shall there be any pain or disease.'
– Something like that as mud sucked at my shoes.

I watched the watchers. But when ropes ran to inter
you there I saw a brown leaf give under a tear. . . .

Now it is autumn and rain. Big drops you can trace.
I notice how one drop's enough to tear
an amber leaf out of the brittle trees.
I suppose much the same happened last year,
but it's now I notice, watching a caricature
of your face glooming over me as I stare
out of the window where the puddles stir.

The window reflects the galleon of fire still,
yards off in the dark, some useless knick-knack.
Rain drips regularly from the loose tile.
A wren ruffles the feathers round its neck,
sheltering in the gutter from the muffled knock
of continual rain. . . . Time to draw the blinds.
The galleon vanishes. A leaf zigzags as it lands.

The Fragments

'My life must be Christ's broken bread,
My love his outpoured wine,
A cup o'erfilled, a table spread
Beneath his name and sign,
That other souls refreshed and fed
May share his life through mine.'

Now they've returned by post the book of hymns
you gave me. It stands narrow among mine,
gold-backed and ribbed like bamboo-cane,
cleaner than the rest. You and your horn-rims
weren't given to read a line.
This music now and again

comes by me. Sometimes the words fill my head;
they speak with my desires but not your hope.
I try to change them for lines you haven't read.
With books you couldn't cope.

'Grief fills the room up of my absent son . . .'

They bring back evenings of study in my room.
Chords rolled from the organ keys you spanned,
the whole house empty. You couldn't read a bar,
only the tune and an octave's occasional boom.
Sometimes I couldn't stand
those wrong notes. They'd jar
your loneliness against me. I'd come downstairs
and make your supper and we would sit and eat
in silence separated by your stumbling airs,
and our eyes would not meet.

'He talks to me who never had a son . . .'

Erratic clack of typing rackets through
my room. Two-fingered my slow hands,
like feelered insects, pick at the crowded keys.
The duet, solos for two.
(A miner, trapped by land-
slide, tapping on his knees
to contact rescue.) But you're the buried one.
I know the ways between us, the walls and loosestrife;
letters unposted, journals in unison.
I'm the resurrection and the life.

'"He that would gain his life shall lose it . . ."'

– '"Being in the form of God, he thought
it not robbery to be equal with God
but made himself of no reputation and took
upon him the form of a servant and was brought

to the likeness of man . . ."' Your odd,
toby-jug figure shook:
'". . . and fashioned as a man he humbled himself and became
obedient unto death, even the death
of the cross. Wherefore God hath given him a name . . ."'
And then you'd gasp for breath.

Straw-light stuffing poked from the bare light.
Crumpets of foam topped each icicled glass.
You entered the bar to sell your magazines
around the mellow; when they claimed their right
to hymns from bible-class,
recalling childhood scenes,
I watched your hands fumble out some harmony.
You offered me your box. Coins would chink
in silence and you whisper:
'"He that hath no money
come ye to the waters and drink . . ."'

6,000,000 Guinness drunk every day . . .

And now I watch my hands fumble the keys,
my type no better than your tunes – those short,
incurving little fingers, the family trait,
never to make the furthest stretch with ease.
How they skew and contort
to type at any rate . . .
Downstairs the strumming guts of guitars
and gramophones replace your wheezing tunes.
I watch acquaintances head for various bars.
The docile bus-queue moons.

I watch them stand solemnly in that queue,
loaded with goods, without grimace or smile.
You'd handled them with tracts and pious books.
You'd always made out something you could do . . .

And now I watch them file
to see some film that looks
once more into the concentration camps.
This, how their victims queued, some accounts said.
Night falls. My face projects in the glow of lamps.
They move about my head.

6,000,000

Radium Therapy

Deflated of flesh,
like axe-hafts,
the shinbones poke from rumpled bedding.

I hurry past
to avoid the radiation field.
The sweat and stench would make one retch.

But turn
to put the blankets straight.
And, leaning through the field,
I warm myself a little in my haste.

from HAVING NO ALTERNATIVE

> 'The sun shone, having no alternative, on the nothing new . . .'
>
> Beckett: *Murphy*

Meeting

I would hardly have remembered your face
but then you used that strange word 'wayzgoose'
and it didn't seem out of place
in your Chinese-miniaturist choice of words.
Heard once it stayed in mind as your monogram,
recalled your Irish voice.

Then you left town
and I had this
as a memory of you,
this odd, misleading sound
for your mediaeval feasts of beer.

Returned unexpectedly after a year
you discovered someone relishing a word
you thought your own,
and in sheer delight now
you make him one to drink with here
but never bring to mind
how oddly this introduction was done . . .

Your dragonfly mind
hovered where seconds flower.

Courtesy Visit

In the small hours –
the din of voices in my ears –
you storm the stairs.

You reach my room for sanctuary
and drum upon the door,
then ram.

Almost in sleepwalk I open up.
You slump in,
weak, scarcely awake.

We turn the lock against them,
make Darjeeling,
black as you like it.

Cheeks veined with spider mauves,
your eyes blink slowly like fish mouths.
No muscle moves.

You've been on the drugs again.

The Terms

If I should suddenly hear that you were ill,
arrested or in need, I'd try to come
as soon as possible. And yet by rail
it still would take a day to reach your room.

If I should suddenly hear that you were ill
your letter would have taken a day to come.
You might be dead before I had the mail,
or die the day I travelled to your room.

And if I were unexpectedly taken ill,
I wouldn't write and trouble you to come
because I know you couldn't help, nor fail
to worry in your dark and curtained room.

This is our friendship. But still
you fled, maybe from this, and must have come
to fidget round some sleazy digs or jail
somewhere unknown . . . or lie dead in your room.

You used to turn up suddenly with a will
in any old street. I miss the way you'd come,
that duffel winged out like a hawk, and hail
me through the traffic. Now streets are dumb.

Thinking of Writing a Letter

Now if I had your address what could I write?
I've seen the shots a cancer patient needs
towards the end. You drift incurably ill,
and your suffering must be worse, the drugs you take.

Suppose I said it's raining here tonight;
shared drinking yarns; sized up rival creeds;
let on I think of easy ways to kill
myself – but pills, not knives, the quarry lake.

They'd need courage. – Cold comfort that would make
in your despair. So I suppose I'd fill

some sheets with quotes, a rhyme, retort or slight
to draw you on to cap one of my leads.

And you would quote again that Yeats you take
to justify your ways beyond your skill.
Something like: 'Whatever flames upon the night
Man's own resinous heart has fed . . .' it reads.

I see England mapped before me, dark and still,
and for a moment point after point of light
from every room you ever left succeeds
across it. The last melts out like a flake.

For twenty miles around there is no hill.
Time past for beacons that can reach your sight.
The silence of this water; jagged reeds;
lattice of light that lazy-tongs the lake.

Dear Murphy,

* * *

Separation

Because the night is cold
and I'm warm from your fire
I hurry down the road.

Yet, glancing back,
I see your shadow watching
at the upper curtains.

Before I wave
you turn into the darkened room.

Lullaby

Midges fizz in the dusk,
sky shows through a thin edge of moon,
a bit of honesty.

The night's a dark promise.
I can go no further with you now;
child, you must sleep.

Steps

I glance in at the open door
to see if my light disturbs you,
head and shoulders out of the covers,
abandoned, comfortable.

The sleeping beauty of children –
my mother's comment –
gushes over my childish head,
stalls my shadow on the floor.
I inch the door to.
Sudden dark might wake you.

Starting your Travels

You try to outstare the journeying dark
but lights burst in heliographs that blind
your sleep-disfocused eyes:
a row of uprights falling to a car's
raking beams – like dominoes in file
or ranks in a cross-fire.

The twin booms of light splinter like bars
of glass across your eyes. You look aside:
a horde of manoeuvring lights,
some market town in cover of the scarp.
That embrous mercury haze across the night
the way our route must lie.

Yet rest now, child. I see shapes in the stars.
And when you wake from dream in a few nights
for terror of the light
closing in round you from the black-moss dark
I shall know how to comfort you in time
and it shall comfort you in time.

Damages

Red-admiral flickering by the cherry tree.
I saw those markings last when still a boy,
and shout, too sharply perhaps, for you to see –
afraid insecticides may soon destroy
the last before you see your first one drift
among the phlox and sideslip, dither, lift.

And, dropping toys, you hurry to my room
fearfully fast and stand almost in tears.
(It's darning up the garden, bloom to bloom.)
I point and out you dart. It nears, then veers,
now poises like a gnomon. Caught in the end.
You bring it me dead; its wings I cannot mend.

Thwarted, I try to explain calmly, brush
the vivid dust from your hands. Still you insist
it fly again, persist, and will not hush
until my angry tone conveys the gist
of death. Silenced, you give me the crumpled wings;
I shelve them with your heap of broken things.

But not till bedtime dare you bring the car,
Buick Riviera with plastic conduction lights,
dropped, when I'd called you, on its towing bar.
You have the pieces. I say I'll put it right.
The tears delayed this morning drop as I take
the glowing plastic glue will turn opaque.

Sleep well.
                    Your toys, my books cobble the floor.
There's that Lagonda I bought myself as a boy.
Toys to repair clutter my desk and drawers.
Irreparably damaged some you most enjoy.
Here since you insist on repairs. Instead,
my words and promises litter your head.

Your strength beyond your skills, so fast you grow;
I cannot clear the backlog of things you break.
More complex now your gifts; already, though,
technology in your toys outstrips me. I make
this pile, your broken marvels, forgotten, outgrown.
My words and ways you may not so simply disown.

Full Circle

Same book. Last year the reader's throat grew dry,
the meaning garbled till the mood was lost
on all the rest in boredom. This time I'll read
the ending out: their prison-ship is tossed
against the rocks of home; one friend must die
saving the younger just as both are freed
from chains by storm to grasp the chain of hands
that friends reach out across the years and sands.

'Greater love . . .' Yes. Even that quote.
That faithful girl has kept a light lit there
for seamen in such straits! Now home, the dead
hero is laid out on the table where
he once had laid his son in death. And note:
the son adopted mourns the father dead –
a careful symmetry. And one attends
them, grey-haired now, not knowing his old friends.

– I ham it up. The seniors I overlook
glance up from private study, grin: the course
they did two years ago. They catch my eye
but other eyes are reddened by the force
of words, and blinkered by their tears to the book,
for hero's death when nearly home and dry;
for one, after long exile returned. Neat,
unlikely, a vicious circle so complete.

Lump in the throat. Yet not for hero friends,
still less for home that circles round once more,
nor for the woman who could wait so long
for love; but for impossibilities of this order,
coincidences needed to shape these ends –

seniors listening now; for kids so strongly
moved by the frame of life prefigured there.
– The seniors already know it will not wear.

Finis. And silence. Time to break this spell.
Seniors laugh off the mood remembered, lame
laughter the kids can hardly understand.
Try questions. No one answers. Pick a name.
A laugher or a quiet one? . . . The bell.
And out they file too quietly. A handful
of seniors asks how many times the book
comes round. Half-smiling, I answer with a look.

Thirty Summers

Clouds shift; the shadows fall
Stallion-gloss of sunlight
on a bough-back.

Clouds shift; the leaves rustle.
I wait for that sun-shaft
to light there again.

Terrace

A terrace of tulips
colourful as a crowd.
What they need
is a match to watch.

Will this old tabby do,
sleeping in the sun?

Crowd

Come away from crowds,
you fool;
why do you hang about?
If she should turn up now
she would be old.

That one is like her, dark,
long hair,
strong stride, unshaken calf . . .
Unfaithful eye,
recharge the memory.

Old Poet on a Rainy Day

FOR DAVID JONES

My old acquaintances and peers,
once allied in the lonely art
and rivals in our riper years,
gather together now on shelves
after so sure a life apart
and peace becomes their books, themselves.

Wait and See

This is the bar you said where we could meet.
I take the corner opposite the door,
prepared to wait
and half-resigned to sit
with one glass for an hour.

Each time a figure darkens the window
I watch the door. And for a moment
a head takes on that bob of yours,
a leg your casual lope,
and I am drawn by you
to several other women.

Tangibles

It was one of those autumn days,
you said,
as if they were consecutive,
distinct yet somehow comparable
as the misty shimmer in each pearl
around your throat.
And so I remember it was –
the crack of apple,
the tang of juice in the teeth
and your hands
always cold to first touch.

Country Walk

I've wound it many times
around my fingers,
that scroll of your hair
fumbled over by the breeze.
It will carry these buttercups
and more.

Masses of buttercups
blacken the grass
until we walk unsteadily
a sky of shaking stars.

Down to earth
in our old spinney,
the sun a hole charred in the boughs,
you reach across me
seeking a leaf of every green
till I catch
in the tips of your hair
a spectrum of stars.

The Swifts

The swifts are back,
their flight on a knife-edge.
In the dusk we watch them
and feel at peace.
Their grace we take
for confirmation.

Our swifts are back,
we say, and touch now.
But their grace survives them,
whichever were ours.
And it hurts to touch you,
that wing of hair.

Whose love, my love,
in my hands tonight?
Whose spring again
in the bounce of your hair?
Our love is ghosted;
our swifts return.

Silver Birch

A delicacy of white feathers
that can cut the hand
rising out of the mist.
One bough the leading edge
of a swan's wing raised for flight.

My hands could span the trunk
arched into darkness
like your throat
thrown back in love.

One dusk when mist returns,
walk along this way, love,
gather an inkling,
my angle of you,
your head thrown back.

Presence

Shadow of a bird in flight
across my window
jogs my room like a blink.

A whole train of thought gone
as though you with your quiet
had come in and sat down.

Returns

A few silver birches among dark pines
like frozen lightnings. They take us back.

You tried to match your steps to my prints
in the soft earth here, such strides.
You pranced in those days. But look,
I cannot tread again in my last print.
A minute edge crumbles like those cliffs
at Cromer where we walked ten years ago.

The going loosens. I take your wrist once more.
white pressure of my grip expands
more or less the same as when you first
stumbled on these tracks
although I cannot touch you quite again
where once I held you fast.

We cover the same ground.
Your life fits into mine.

Dusk

Moon a sliver of apple
blue on a knife-blade.

Light enough for a known face.
I touch shadow round your eyes.

Gift of Words

That patience of yours,
standing half the morning
to watch a rose you planted bloom.

So long like that, years,
you've waited for me.
I have to watch you always.

Crescent of melon, your bare back
where blouse and jeans have come apart.
The windows between us.

Too impatient to watch your roses,
I want my hands to feel
the equipoise of your hips.

You turn with a spray of roses,
a focus for my room,
fragrant cloud, I think you call them.

The petals will drop silently for days,
scented on these files and folders.
Sometimes I've heard them land.

Crocus

Our old gnarled path.
We're late again this year,
the still flame in our clump
of crocus past its best,
but one, sculptured, fragile,
half an eggshell.

Your head to one side,
your hair heavy and slow,
my plumb-line,
sways to the vertical
as you kneel and try
to purse it up to flame again.

Sleep

As soon as your sleep is sound
I slip my arm from around you.
You can't tell
though you'll dream something up
to explain your loss of warmth.

In the still hours
your cold hands reach for me.

Their gentle pressure
hardly disturbs my sleep.
Unstirring, they become my warmth.

Lullaby

Sleep, love, go to sleep
and I'll watch over you
as I have done these years,
these shadows of curtain haze,
and breathe into your hair
the things we do not say.

You murmur as if you hear
some saying of the day,
and nuzzle the pillow down,
but, tracing an edge of light
along your shoulder line,
my hands touch on your dream.

Hold

That perfect apse,
your fingers with their curvature.
They hold a stillness
I can't touch.

Tentative
your hands sense out
for things as if air
lay denser round them.

Mine
that undo things for you
would leave their mark.

Love,
it's not much
but it's something
we hold together.

Lost and Found

The warmth of her, unbreathable
as she presses over me
hopelessly scanning the shelves
the only way she knows.

(She asked the time on Westminster Bridge.)
She turns the plants to the sun
and she is looking for a map of the district.
I round on her – like a moth.

Old Haunt

Scotch fir, the trunk
staked in the still pools of its boughs
on the old hill.

The needles kill the grass
where we left our shapes
so long ago.

Their criss-crossings
crazed your bare legs.
You tried for a fern pattern.

This stillness was there then;
boughs like green snow overhanging;
and the peace was no trouble to us.

Two Sparrows

They take off squabbling
and loop each other
like a flying bolas –
and their shadows.

Time to see it happen:
our hands like that now
when they skirmish to manoeuvre
in open tenderness.

Gifts

More books,
that dress I thought was you,
worn once,
another pen to try my hand.

We're down to gifts now,
mine against yours,
and each more costly than the last.

They hang fire about us everywhere.

Meander

Dark meander of hair
a river between banks of snow
and my touch lasting
like a snowflake in its course.

Keeper

Something about you that might break,
a hand's turn,
delicate as a figurine,
caught and held me.

Something small and terrified
sheltered in the verve of your eyes
like a silver fox,
nocturnal, svelte.

A lull in the talk,
the dark suddenly noticeable
and the odd glance
of something too timid to tame.

The sight grows rarer, love.
It keeps more and more from me.
My old night-farer,
let it still live.

Retrospect

Wanting some yourself
you offer me cherries.
Girlish again
you hang a pair over your ear
pale where they touched
as your breasts were.

Wanting memories
you hold out a wishbone stalk
to split between us.

But I want my time back.
Give me back
the pressure of my hands.

Tie

A marbling of fine veins
across your right temple,
the skin opalescent.
Blood too near the surface.

Truce

In your play which was no play
the knife glanced my arm,
a red mouth opened mute.
A fortnight's casual conversation
out of that,
now healed to a scar.

Twilight

Dusk
lit by a bowl of roses
and your hand white, so white
against the oak table,
poses a peace I know only by sight.

Dark to you always
my hands seemed closer once
than nocturnes in black and white
those nights your shoulders gleamed,
that mane of shadow down your back.

Deadlock

Nothing more irritating
when the hands are engaged
than a trickle of liquid
like an insect running down the face,
rain or sweat or even blood.

You want me to take your hand in mine
and will not want to dry your eyes
until I do,
though I will wait
until you fall asleep.

Impasse

Your eyes closed on me.
Your drift always against my drive.
I draw your scalp back by the hair
to lift the lids.

And by the time they do
I shall have gritted my teeth
into a smile for you.

Retraction

Your overnight bag gone;
so much left behind:
you tried to keep everything.

I go over again in black
the words I wrote to you
or underscored in red.

The flourishes defeat me,
the dab hand
has lost its cunning.

The red shows through.
I'll send them on.
Retraction enough.

Insight

For sight like an ophthalmoscope,
once it was a wish,
now what a hope,
to penetrate the leaf-light
of your green iris
to the shadow-play beyond.

The dark can take you now
for all a shaft could show:
a room of gipsy flowers
and potted plants,
the ten-mirror echo
of your defensive laugh.

Keepsake

You call me to you
kneeling over a single crocus
under the oak.

Your scroll of hair
now screening the steady flame,
some secret you'd have unique:

These three impressures
inset within the petal,
fluted, concave, minute.

How long we'd keep this insight in season,
you said,
as ours, strong as a vow.

But I have held that moment:
you leaning,
your hair scrolled around your shoulders . . .

And now this clump of crocus
hidden a moment in time,
its saffron blinding.

The Mind's Eye

Curls that should jingle with your slightest move –
I might have known you'd soon be back,
your next shift
to trouble the mind's eye.

Naked, or dressed to kill.
But clothed – that's new.
I watch the passes that you make,
your hands slow-motioning to save a glass.

Your skirt deflating like a parachute,
you kneel and tilt your head
to catch the glint of fragments littering the floor.

That skirt's a laugh,
and just to pique you more
I'm going to make you last like that
and unaware before me on your knees.

Those curls will jingle at your slightest move –
After-image, my after-love, look up.
You're still my only source of feeling.

Eidetic Image

Memory of a girl laughing,
your hair a fall of flame,
gold burning down
and shadow flickering up,
head to one side
like a bird listening.

Pose of an advert now –
mirror enough for you at last –
you get at me from all angles.

I don't know how widespread you are
but I expect you everywhere.
And at this distance alone reflect –

nostalgia if you like –
that maybe you never posed this one before,
a girl laughing in her glass
without your famous poise,
the shadow flickering up,
the gold burning down.

Obsession

I bear you in mind always – white
as balsa wood your body was.
You were all women once to me.

The blade of shadow down your thigh,
it's pretty common; some of your ways
I love in other woman I meet.

I've assembled them all tonight,
all dressed to kill and all to watch
your private strip; it's your big scene.

I bare you in the mind's eye
so make it hot and strong for once;
they'll take your fine points off, my sweet.

Vigil

Now you are gone
your small perfections inveigle me:
curve of your eye-lid closed in sleep
widens to my horizon.

Sleepless
I used to watch those pupils move,
shifting deltas of blue veins,
blindly scanning my face.

Some nights I came near,
my lips in touch
with your pulsing lids
to catch the drift of your dream.

Wildflower

Crushed fragrance
and a few flower heads
bend to the light
out of my footprints –
purple florets,
established, wild,
encroaching underfoot.

How long ago it must have been
you told me the local name
for something much like this,
if I remember it,
in those days
when what your hands touched
was my life.

From *Cross-Channel*

Recognition

Face once loved,
so constant in the mind,
I could have passed you anywhere
not knowing who you were.

Rain

All morning long now, missing you,
I sit and watch the summer rain
falling, ticking through the shrubs
against the window – white blooms.
You would know their country names,
these flowers you would never cut.

And there beneath the leaves that give
some delicate filigree of grass,
blunt pencil's double line its stem.
One drop would break it down if hit.
But minutes of this time have passed
and not a drop has nicked it yet.

The tip-down of a neighbouring leaf
gives it a momentary, brushing shock –
one bulging drop about to fall,
left globed upon its filigree.
The leaf recoils, smashes the drop.
The rain pours. I watch that stalk.

You would know its country name.
You always knew what to call
those unseasonable costly sprays
I brought to make your tears my fault.

Unspoken

This ache always to bring you
a gift to last some time
and yet I know
how this would go beyond the drift
of our arrangement:
flowers or food,
wine to persuade a share of mood.
That's how we've got it made.

And anything much beyond these
would be in time the gift for loneliness
and let you press the same on me,
some token lasting thing
until all we have now,
these late daffodils,
would somehow be over.

One Another

A SONNET SEQUENCE

The Lane

The willows hang their yellow swarms across
the turning by the hump-back bridge – that lane.
I still can make the river wash and swirl,
sucking the stonework underneath, and feel
pocking the wall-top the green grit of moss.
Like scratches down old movies, a thin rain.
No one turned there, not even boy and girl
in all the years I passed. It's almost real.

I shan't walk now along that nameless lane.
(Only the memory pays for local maps.)
No face or place in the village to take me back.
Posit: the first aerial, then the stack,
a few houses expecting no one perhaps,
a child wondering away, nose to the pane.

Landscape

Me peeling away at a loose end of bark,
the silver birches; there, the stunted one,
a run of silver paint on rough grained wood,
and underfoot the usual dumping ground.
That childish hope when this was more a park
to peel some silver off and catch the sun
or make a mirror. Never any good.
But here's a trunk my hands can still surround.

Me peeling away at a loose end still,
watching the darkness grow beneath my hand,
scorched earth, scorched earth, and, staring in my face,
the old landscape I thought I left at will.
– Eyes, eyes that bear in mind this meagre land,
look back; hold me stronger than the place.

Dissolve

Face of a Greek tyro, and the neat hair
a cap of sparrows' wings, the lean thigh
in motion scooped and fluted, midriff bare –
I look for what it is that takes my eye,
and wish you deftest screw and steady aim
for no good reason but the longbow curve
your leg has, tensed; supply you with a name,
moth to a flame, that dark central reserve.
A sleepless night I had of it, your taut
body still poised to cue, your face, that face
pursuing, not pursued, in every thought.
And then a name clicked back into its place.
    Hard, to recall how long ago things last,
    my love, old love, my stand-in for the past.

Response

Dear, I should like you once in your life to be moved
by a printed phrase, not for the writer's sake,
still less for mine, but so that you could say
for once how odd it feels to learn your mood,
your feelings nursed along so nice and lush,
are nothing private to speak of, nor quite fresh,
my love, my dearest love. Though do not fret
yourself; there's something here to like or lump:

The dead tabby's paw clatter on the glass
when rain or shadow trick the eye, odd times,
can shake me more than what the mind replays
of one with her Shetland-pony fringe and glance,
or, worse, the moccasin-slouch, palm-forward style,
of that one from my student days, the plague.

Cone

Not dearest, but the nearest I have come
to love, such as it is, I'll watch you read,
your urchin hair within the lamp-light's cone,
the spray arrested on those curls that screen
your face. I always fell for that, but more
a street-light's cone, I don't know why, in rain,
an auburn head, the storm's panicky Morse,
the lamp-light and a moment's ambered grace.

No, don't look up, my love, nor ask with eyes
what if we had our time again. Read on,
calves under thighs, your knees like new loaves,
and let me see you read my thoughts tonight:
the busby neatness of that auburn gone,
our destination dark and undisclosed.

Dialogue and Soliloquy

'Let's talk about the roses. They don't hurt,
do they? Red, spiky – red or maroon?
Soft, aren't they soft? And quite inert.
And look, there, look: the silly old moon
gormlessly dithering like a kid's balloon
left on a pond. That cloud making it spurt.
The darkness comes. Let's talk about it soon.
A snug fit, a shade closer than your skirt.'

– I am the apple of his inner eye.
He wants to core me and he bores me, bores.
Once in a blue moon I'm two in his sky.
Cowish, I jump them for him on all fours.
I'm strip lighting and he wants it stark:
'Nearest, you come no closer than the dark.'

A Little Light

Once it was a touch and then a tone of voice
and always promise of a turn of mind.
I could have touched your lashes any time
and you not bat an eyelid nor recoil.
Such calm. Your trust was always hard to take.
We've colonized a space now, an arm's reach,
filled with the things we touch on, books I need,
the plants you tend, green-fingered, self-contained.

Pressure, a touch, it never took much to work;
gentleness, warmth, the shadow mask on eyes
that give back nothing but a little light.
You turn from me, you grope for timeless words
and my dumb hands go out to you in time
to hold, like a flower's scent, your mind in mine.

The Rose

Such concentration on a single rose,
you look as though you watch it breathe the scent
till I am watching you and held intent,
your breath so hushed it hardly comes or goes.
What does it say to hold you in that pose,
that my lips cannot move, my hands invent?
Your words, they never tell me what is meant;
my hands can't touch the peace your body knows.

Pale bloom that gathers light from dusk, your hand
as white as whittled hazel without shine,
the sill and window where you hold quite still.
A word could break the spell. . . . I ache to stand
in for your eyes and grasp this rose in mine
as closely as your hand along the sill.

Insights

When shall we ever know each other more
than you this rose or me this quietude
of yours that breathes a presence through the room,
your slightest movement making stillness clear
as flickers of the firelight do. You pore
over the vase. You wouldn't know my mood,
nor I your insight to a rose's bloom;
your rose a focus, mine a misting sphere.

Move, love; finger the petal fallen there.
(Your palate's curvature, its touch to me.)
Now feel the micro-hesitance and know
the sense my hands have of your skin – your hair,
more like, that rounds their roughness in its flow.
So touch the rose, and in my hands you'll be.

Record

It is her microphone. She speaks with powers
I do not hear, no movement on her lips.
Dumb rose, record her thoughts, her fingertips
for after-comers. Make her the language of flowers.
– No, no, she listens. Others murmur here.
This is the poise that I have never caught.
To let go of a rose as of a thought,
the bloom untremored as her hand lifts clear.

Are roses still becalmed where Helen is?
The trees drop shadows; light ripples the leaves.
That time, held frame, of shadeless memories;
the light like glass. Oh, love, you turn again.
If only we let go as your hand reprieves
a rose, unmarked, and the daylight could be plain.

Talisman

Bellflowers, seldom seen now, stellar, trim,
on porcelain where the day is warm and clear
as flame within a candle's melting rim;
that squirl so delicately fellowed here.
– The trinket-well I gave you long ago
to cast a wistful spell that was your own.
And it became you, love. But now it's broken,
my clumsy hands: the light flawed with a mote.

It hurts, as if a talisman, now drained,
withdrew its gentle aura from you, though
you're just the same and do not seem aware.
But here's the perfect match at last obtained.
Throw out the first and who would ever know?
Yet no two days of summer make a pair.

Match

Someone who loved the clay and loved the flowers
made this and caught the look of day in it.
Not one who tried to see how exquisite
it was in loving me and my sad hours.
The broken one I'll save as rightly ours
and you will sometimes see me watch that split
and blur it out with wondering how we knit
our days together with such clumsy powers.

Someone who loved me gave this broken thing
and I will match it with the perfect one.
These two shall be for us a perfect match:
one past and one to come, as time may bring.
And since we don't know which of them is done
we may move gently and perfection snatch.

Silence

Cloud stilted along on two great spokes of light.
And then to enter the room, its shadow cool.
A bowl of roses, the oak-table, white blooms
like slow swans reflected in its pool, plumes
brushed by a moment's breeze. A dusty gold
fizzing a shaft of sun, the mullion's shade
leading across the carpet – shoulders bare,
shadowed by a great silence of cascading hair,

the woman sitting, focused within her mind,
(myself unseen) hands folded in her lap
cupping the darkness loosely like a bird,
book on the floor accordioned.

To find you there,
presence to presence. Cloud happens to change
the light. You turn as though you heard it move.

Declination

That momentary declination of your head,
the water-chevron hairs along your nape,
revive an old attraction. I slowly drape
your shoulders, hold you there. You turn instead
your baffled squirrel look – and nothing said,
all lost. My love, some day I'll buy a cape
and every time your hair's in its great shape
I'll help you on with it to bow that head.

What binds us, dearest, is this touching grace.
It's like a cat's or in a squirrel's leap.
Or else, for me, the glossing of a beech.
But you know the dodge, the time and place.
I have to eavesdrop on your style of sleep –
your eyelids close and you are out of reach.

Aubade

Our hands have had their say time and again:
your quiet touch, the cat in the dog's shade,
a sneaking stroke of love in the shopping parade,
some grasp of shared experience in pain.

Dark in my long watch of your summer sleep,
I wonder what my hands would have to say
the day you die. And all the words that weigh
into the head make my flesh and blood creep

to you to wrest you closer from the night.
– Sleep on, my love, sleep in your cool bed.
May these cold hands never enter your head.
And in the morning may the breaking light
suffuse your lids with rose before you wake.
The first shadow on you my touch will make.

Shadow

Shadow of a leaf on a butterfly's wing,
solid as a beetle's wing-case, fine veneer.
I wait to hear it click down like a spring

the instant that the tortoise-shell flits clear.
I'm learning to be patient, love. You freeze.
My hold is less than light on you, that sheer

absorption, as you tense for flight or breeze.
Glacially, you edge forward now. I know
enough of you to see you mean to ease

your shadow over the wing and hold it so.
That daft stray lock of yours will almost reach.
You cannot make it stay. It's touch and go.

The shadow leaf snaps down in me like a screech.
I catch you off balance and without speech.

View

So much, so much . . . I only have to reach
my hand to you, my fingers swaying the fine
hair of your nape as the breeze that field of wheat.
You hardly notice, though there comes to mind
a gentle lulling. And this pressure to hold
your mind to instances of mine – it seems
almost enough. These hands can trail a shoal
of lights along your hair and you will sleep.

And I would hold the gift of sleep for you.
No other gift so good, unless some tact
were in my hands to press on you the mood
of this great purple thunder-bank, flint-knapped
along the brink with light, or to attune
my sense of music to your stone-calm hands.

Music

Full of mortal longing the cor-anglais yearns.
I thought of Chatterton, the marvellous boy,
at least that painting in the Tate, the light
there, or that *April Love*, the rich mauves,
the light there much the same, as she half turns
and looks inward. Her song would surely cloy.

An English wood and autumn burning late,
the boat-knock branches as the light breeze moves,
those kipper-coloured leaves and, feather-frail,
one poplar. The pile of this moss so smooth,
so cool to stroke. A squirrel, brown, ears frayed,
quizzical; sun enough to make him muse.

His reaper sang contralto in this cadence.
Will no one tell me what she hears, my music?

Her Concentration on a Nutshell

They used to make us cockleshells for the bath.
You open them so gently, knife down the seam.
Uncrinkle the kernel, though. What worlds of earth
would round out from the walnut; not the same,
oh, not the same as ours! Another scale.
The mind it is, inside the head. (He'd like
to crack my codes, edge deep into the skull.)
I part the hemispheres with a nuclear click.

Colour of blanched almond, these firm thighs,
and curved the same where they surface in the bath.
This English pallor, smooth and hazed. – All space
is curved and he has reached his bound in these.
He wants me all and he can have them both.
Come, tan of walnut juice, you add some spice.

Pressed

These flowers are a gentleness in my grasp.
My hands harbour the haft-hold too long,
their lightest drift to you a weathered rasp.
These slight flowers give as the wind grows strong.

This wide reach of evening, all that surf
of cloud-rack, the thunder-bank's great rift,
the rayless sun no more than a clean pine kerf.
Flowers and hand one shadow on the drift.

See, we could press them there against your skin
and mine, mementos of our day – though much
the better in a book. Words always win.
We'd have to stay like this all night in touch.

Love, in your most private grief, my hands
have never touched you without desire to have.

Sunset and Storm

Cool grass-blades creep up and over my hand.
The old blaze of sunset deepens the thunder-bank
on green-tops wet with light, liftless, tranquil.
All's said and done, my love. You understand,
the years I have assumed, this peace before storm.
(Eye blinked by the wingless flight-phase of a bird.)
This wait that never varies for leaves stirred
by the first gust, the first rain, chill, enormous.

Too long I've let these things speak for me.
I can survive only as long as your mind.
Hold instances of mine. This bracelet of bone
that splays your hand in the drenched grass. You're free.
Go in. Wash off the mud. But leave behind
the link of skin that binds you in your own.

Deed of Gift

It's not enough. Not personal enough.
Landlubbers all have fallen for this time.
Something that pulls the mind up sharp like a lime
I need, none of this sentimental stuff.

I'll give you a pendant watch. It's not much
but wear it always under your blouse to tell
a moment you can only show yourself.
It will take your breath away, cold to the touch.

I'll clip the catch for you. Nod down your neck,
hold still. But my hands, love, are cold, so cold.
There now. Your pulse is beating the time told.
I promise you'll only hear the odd second

like a skipped beat: my hands chill on your nape
and your thin skin cringing up like crape.

Shades

My hand's reach larger than life upon the blind,
the light so limited that the dark leaks in.
You shudder at the shape in mind, you say;
a branch wuthered against the window, bare,
hag-black to stifle you – until my hand,
soft as a shadow, brushes away your cry.
Dark promises, my love, lie candid there.
I've just the ghost of a touch to sidle down

your spine. Once a shadow, always a ghost.
Remember among windswept oaks or cloistral beech
these hands. They'll haunt your body mostly there.
How they'll remember at arm's reach you comb
    and slowly comb your hair until it gleams
    satisfactorily with my sweat. Sweet dreams.

Moon

These hands are so old. I don't know what to think.
They hold their own when I have lost my grip.
They know of ways around that you let slip.
You tremor like water just above the brink.

I watch your face for thoughts, for mood – your face
wizened a moment by movements soft as time.
Look, love, I'll gather what your features mime.
Your eyes reflect a light I cannot place.

Now you are young again. In the low light
your skin-tone has the mother-of-pearl that blurs
the rimless moon in mist. That's the rare sight
you always bring to mind now, though you smile:
and what if that means frost and heavy furs?
You'd lie there still, my love, in all your style.

Frost

White crystals clear, lean over, melt away
as breath peels back along the frosted fence.
Moss-feints return. The wonder is all day
whether the grain, the green, will be as dense
when dusk returns, or white again with frost,
clinging like iron-filings, to the wood.
Again he breathes his warmth, all focus lost,
until the knot nets outwards as it should.

– So much you bring back as you bend, your hair
brushing the frost, and breathe to melt the white
upon a spider's web, taking good care
to break no thread. More frost, my love, tonight.

Like kids, my lips will melt a frost tonight,
a frost and frost of light along your lids.

Hand and Head

I sweat it out, your perfume in the heat;
the closest we have come, and dear enough
without this hankering for the deeper stuff.

And yet to know you like an open book,
my lost language never glossed completely.
You turn over again to a clean sheet.

Just once, perhaps, to read of my approach
under the cover of your sharpest look-out
calmly anticipated nook by nook.

In these arms also your need of surprise,
a stroke of genius rather than encroachment,
the craft say, of this fronded silver brooch.

'King Alfred ordered me made.' How neat it lies,
a starry blur above foreshortened thighs.

The Shadow

She promised all. You gave me what you had:
your stillness centripetal to a room,
your gawky poise coaxing a rose to bloom,
barefoot, your heel-down, ballerina pad.

And yet you can't compete within her shadow.
In dreams, in anger, she surfaces, assuming
a sleeking otter-back of naked grooming
under the nylon, its flowing off so gradual.

Breast turning a propeller of light, she straddles
her stole, manoeuvring for the slowest zoom-in.
That once you stalked off in the pine-dark gloom
and she turned up in only your old plaid.

Bare, with your heel-down, ballerina pad,
your bird-launching laugh, how she skedaddled!

A Long Shot

Mad hikes over bracken, nettle-beds, wildflowers
to find a place no foot had trodden first.
I swore I'd remember every single hitch
but in the end you were too many for me.
You always were impossible. A place all ours,
there must be one, you say.
                                                  A struck tree,
the boggiest corner, midges at their worst,
its riven trunk straddled across the ditch.

Just as it fell, you say, the storm last night.
You have to walk on it in your high heels.
Your flared skirt of blinding saffron peals
this way and that, my silent bell. One stone,
then you strap-hang on a willow, a real sight.
Hold it.
                    And here you stand on tips of bone.

The Thunder Stone

Ten years and no memories to call our own,
you say, eyes scavenging across the field,
raking the sky-line for something it might yield.
(Basket creak of leaves by the dry-stone.)
Let's find a gap that no one else has known
and get an angle frost or wind revealed,
then with a seeded handful of earth concealed –
or cones, my sparrows drying off, windblown.

– No, here's a chalky flint I split on flint;
our landscape on its surface and, inside,
these mirror-image, thunder-purpled skies.
All glint, and water will restore the glint.
They'll never fade to blue. This one we'll hide,
the other take – a match that never lies.

Storm

Your fear of lightning, my need of the storm.
The great pylons a pale shadow of the cloud
bouldered above us and your slight figure cowed.
Sky cracks like ice and the rain slow and warm.
Your hand in mine. I cannot hold your fear
and you can't draw the need from me, your head
so close I muffle up your other ear.
The two of us, you say, the two of us dead.

The power to drive a city in that flash,
all spent to burn a vacuum in the sky.
I watch it branch and you tense for the crash.
Big drops darken and connect across your dress.
Love, where we hold close we are bone-dry;
you cling, and what comes through is powerless.

Walk

I know, I know. It is only a dream,
but there are dogleg rivers I cannot cross
and paths in company I walk alone:
a certain tilt of willow, a touch of moss.
Yet still there come these moments when you seem
some distance with me in the placeless zone –
unless I catch sight of the knurled bough
angling the path I cannot quite say how.

Though, love, you must have paths and paths to walk.
How you might need my hand to bring you through.
(That flint split to a sky of thunder grey.)
And you might reach for me as now you do
and say: 'That's betony, that broken stalk,
and that chink-chink's a thrush. They fix the day.'

Bird's Eye

We take an hour off in the watery sun.
Bird's-eye, you suddenly exclaim: minute,
a tiny pansy-type of a bleak blue.
I actually like the thing, the way it shuns
the eye, less brash than pansies.
Not the name,
you say, my mother called it that. You find
the name. It must be in the books.
I'll try,
love, though we know it's just to pass the day.

I'll find its name, and it will be the name
of that nothing we did to say we lived.
But bird's-eye, let the children say
until, when grown, they find its grassy dip
and wonder over what its true name is.
– Birsy, love, the flower I cannot change.

Memento

A leaf. He's given me an autumn leaf,
faded, but never to perish with the fall.
The marvels of technology! Every least
serration, every vein and slightest fault
precisely sealed in burnished copper foil,
and yet so light. He'd even make a style
of dead leaves. I'll wear it over the void
of my breast. There, leaf to the closest eye.

Funny this catch. . . . And there's a pinpoint leak
the foil has left. The air will seep inside.
Brave new technique, and he has not the skill
this time to mend it. Slowly, slowly, leaf,
you'll sidle out on me, his secret sign,
built-in obsolescence of life under a skin.

One Another

I am that silent pool. I mirror, opaque.
I float the water-lilies, candescent flame,
and I reflect the imperturbable swan.
No cloud-race scuffs my surface; that stake
lays claim to my depths, leaving no wake.
Minnows dart bright silence, the perch aim.
Stones make rings around me and are gone.
I still the rain's trickle. I become a lake.

Her body flows from me in the night.
Like evening mist on a river, she comprehends
the darkness. As blossoms in the mist, the white
to white, my touch floats down to her and ends
somewhere unseen, drifting with the stream.
The fearful silence where dark waters gleam.

Dream

Your presence like a drug that does no harm
cannot enclose me from the trackless night.
Let me sleep now . . . and your pervasive calm.
– Awareness hurtling down a rail of light,
it plummets headlong in the roaring ditch
where bones, a mildew green, clutch out their roots,
and blood seeps from a wound this stolid pitch
of ants that waver to yowls of distant brutes.

Let us rest now, love. The terror will keep.
Only in nightmare is it safe to scream.
All quietudes I have you manage to find;
I will not promise you my share of sleep.
Still waters widen the quiet in your dream.
Let us sleep now; the dark is to my mind.

Compact

For term of life you are determined mine.
Some tree is bound to shadow forth my reach:
no man whose hand has not the same design;
a touch or two of mine you'll have to teach.

And when you seek the years in the window pane,
a dog's claw scuffed along the street will pass
shiver on shiver down your spine again
like these nails scratching down your looking-glass.

And what would you ever do to change the line
your first sleep makes of eyelid into cheek
that you have never seen and I call mine?
This curl behind the ear that spoils your chic?

We are determined, love, for term of life,
and if we fold, it's blade into the knife.

Comfort

The slipping shoulder-strap – yet now with calm
I watch, and, yes, the old impatience still:
your thumb slips in, a neat barge of the arm
and comfort comes again; the slight cups fill
as hands pray backwards in a kid's quick drill:
naked you shiver in your ever green charm.
Such ingrained love of comfort in night's chill!
And then you leap in the dark without a qualm.

My comfort, you, whose comfort used to goad.
How do we do it? Arms in such a twist
all night. They'd cramp in moments if awake.
Sleepy, hoick my arm up over your waist.
Oh love, may such a comfort still hold good
the night your ghosts or mine begin to walk.

Present

This tiny squirrel ornament you chose
    to give me, knowing I love the miniature.
    You mean it for the smoky, bounding creature,
give me grace and lissomness, the fellow's
quizzical look. And, by some lucky chance,
    you have: they've slipped and made one darker pupil
    stare from the head, half-turned, as if the ill-
painted cone had caused him some perturbance.

You want to give all this. And I accept it.
    Cheeky fellow. Look, you couldn't guess
which hand he's in, so sleek and exquisite!
    Yet, love, it's only touches give such softness,
grace . . . though hands, my hands that drowse your passive
shoulders feel more gentleness than they give.

Inklings

I came once on a place where a presence dwelt
that was no vestige of a living thing,
dank and foreboding, like a worldless suffering
condemned to leech into all life it felt;
the sudden brinking of a forest in the dark,
sheer on to silent waters, still as tar.
And now that place moves with me like a scar.

You plant your acorns, say we'll leave a mark.
– Love, let it be. The slant light clings to your hair.
The shadow of a flame, you block the sun.
What inkling of us would you nurture there
to brood upon the waters without form and void?
– You loop a twig and lift a sunset spun
into the trees. You blow. All ghosts destroyed.

Fledgling

That fledgling falls up fluttering to a bough.
I see an autumn leaf reverse, you say;
and spurt ahead – a child making a play
to catch it up, the street forgotten now.

– Oh, love, suppose the mind holds more than sense,
and things we love may bear some lasting trait
of us that later minds may mediate,
something survive where mind once grew intense.

You would return where roses are in bloom,
a concentration round a rose's scent;
or in the spring with swifts to skim and zoom,
and I shall not be there to watch you ache
to enter flower or flight. . . . Now, as you went,
you turn and breast the leaf-light, flake on flake.

Glimpses

Caught in the angle of the steps a shoe brad,
a crushed packet glinted; an ancient pool
of stagnant light wrinkled a tarmac roof.
An odd corner of the casual eye that had
Waterloo Bridge in mind, the pine-shaped, cool
scribbles of light. For days, like a reproof
too trivial to tell, that litter fixed my thought
with every glimpse of mine you'd never caught.

And one seen from a train: a Surrey field,
a crack willow with fishing withes that leant
across a nettled ditch where pollen lay
denting the surface tension. So long concealed
and nothing much to tell: a moment spent
without you, love; the moments build away.

Her Prophecy

Three days after my death I shall return.
I will return and find you not in grief
but lost in quietude now past belief,
gazing upon the frost of patterned fern
across the panes ghosted with mist and trees.
You shall be calm as my oaks ridged with rime,
for all that you could not possess in time
has vanished – haven't I? – with ease.

For now you know there's nothing in the oaks,
nothing of me; there never was. I meant
those steady hands to cup a whorling bud
like life so tight they crushed it into scent.
Your world, that could not be to flesh and blood,
has vanished. Peace be with you – till it chokes.

Hearing the Flowers

There you go. Catch the minutest shudder
of petals in the fire's draught, and there you are,
your book a bird ruffling feathers in air
chilled by the sudden rustle of a shadow.

It frightens me, the mind, where it will shelter.
Sit beside me. Keats, in this fragment here,
more warm and capable to me, toward her,
than in his chosen works. Lean on my shoulder.

We're into words again. You're in my hands.
I'll hold the book for you. Murmur aloud
the living lines the dying hand still haunts;
your head weighs on my heart its mortal load.
You lose the place in shaking out your hair.
My love, it's far too close for flowers in here.

Duotone

Hands, hands to touch me like a sparrow's wings
gliding across a puddle's little sky.

    Gentleness, pressure, closer than murmurings,
    the flesh-tones pearling where my fingers lie.

Suavity, suavity of fingers, skim and plane;
husks of his touch I liquefy – I'm air.

    A shadow blown across a field of grain,
    the drifting of my hands along her hair.

In dream his touch is softer than the dark;
all moods, all modes of thought at the fingertips.

What keeps such softness from my least remark,
gentleness, pressure, speechless on my lips?

Darkness we thought to enter with a torch.

Blind in the night we're dumb from talking touch.

Spectrum

My darling has the rain at her fingertips,
sun in her hair. Steady, she aims to make
a local little rainbow. Time, do not shake
though silver crescents swirl around eclipse,
as watching with wonderful patience here I stand,
considering where on earth the light will break,
coloured with some conviction for her sake.
Soon she will have me drinking from her hand.

You kneel and pick up grains of dust in the swirl
of several drops to make your spectral band.
Love, turn. I catch the spectrum in your hair,
and you, you easily could raise your hand,
arrange those drops of light on the odd curl
and take my word for rainbows in the air.

Clear Stream

The water runs through my fingers, always will.
Remember when I tried to drink from yours?
But you're away again, and the earth scores
your shadow on the run. I watch it spill,
the stain of water dark and shapeless. Hair
that flows like water as you chase or shake
it willowing down. Most taken with the air,
then most you're mine, though hardly for my sake.

Sooner or later you'll come back to cool.
The ground's too wet for anything so bare.
You'll find a way, a cat and water-shy.
How long we'll wait for shade to seep and pool.
Flow like water, my eyes caught in your hair,
our time turning.

Moth-Light

The sun-blaze sinks again and the brittle sky
shells over, yellow, luminescent green.
The light rusts through the black foil of trees,
and a martin zigzagzigs in a last flight.
Shadows, shadows, mindless shadows rise.
The countless times we've lazed till the last gleam
crumbles from the clouds, and it seems peace
we never came to come to us in time.

Your body says it is. Long shadows seep
to you and tide into small pools of shade.
I watch. I watch you watch. So many repeats
and nothing to speak of. The light that studs your eye
is light that glitters in a drop of rain.
light of my eye, you moth-light to the mind.

Dusk

The years in the window pane, the daffodils
leaning stiffly like children's paper windmills
    still toward evening, the mitre buds of lilac.
    Wood-scent your hair was; young, your face looks back.

You start, shivering, at a boy's cry like God
along the street, and watch a girl go slipshod
    in her mother's high heels. Earliest starlight
    and you'd make out new patterns in the night.

And my hand, still dark to white on yours, though wizened.
    Enough now, was it ever enough to hold you,
this touch no words came close to in the end?

Love, leave the crazy tock of moth to window,
    the lamp-light's cone an auburn head shines through.
Catch again the splendour of light in the wine-glow.

The Game

Now don't you fret. There is no other way.
Some time or other there must come an end.
What would you have? And how would it hurt less?
Come on, give me your hand, finish the game.
You'll see how softly I return its Morse.
Then I shall get that good night's sleep
we never had those crazy times your sleek
shadow pranced and frescoed all four walls.

As I came out of darkness and found light,
and found it finer in your lively eye,
so into nothing I shall go and find
the cool moss of darkness was no lie.
I know where to turn. A starlit night;
take one of your walks now. I shan't mind.

Autumnal

Too close we breathe each other's tepid breath.
– The first time it was and meant to stick.
Late afternoon. A shoal of leaves windswept
across the window. You with your lousy gift
for drama: 'The leaves are falling, I must fly.'
Yet stayed to fling the window wide and catch
a leaf or two, then turned with a wet shine,
hair all over the place, one lacquered lash.

Autumn's hamming it up as ever again.
Odd angles like veins, the runnels down the pane.
A leaf with the rain's adhesion clings to the sill
against all gusts. My love, only last year
I willed that leaf to hold. The window chill
against my face, and your name coming clear.

The Oak

More shadow leaves than real on your old oak.
My touch more shadow than the day can clear.
Your face, a shade closer than the lure
of all the living; your body is the dark
beneath my hands. Was there ever light
enough for you? Was light ever enough?
Winter gave most. Now, love, you are the north
my memory steers from, late, so very late.

I cannot uproot an oak. I cannot move
the place I live, the mind derange its fix.
A few dead leaves lift on the aftermath.
We followed the foxgloves where the path forks;
it seems a way we never chose but took.
Now, love, I'm going down the other track.

Before Sleep

Barbaric . . . yet I should have seen you dead,
and quelled the endless images of death
that rise up mouthing speechless from the depth
of time – your hand reaching again, condemned
to splay against a surface-tension stretched
like polythene. Your fingers whiten, press,
like children's noses, for rescue or to fend
me off. Oh make it clear. – There, on the breast,

a vein straggles like a silver birch.
Tell me it's not an image you intend.
Far love, I look with pity for the first
time ever on your body, feel a sense
of treason. It's finished, love. Leave off the frenzy.
We cannot even now be just good friends.

Revenant

My arm around you comforts me at night
that when the ghosts come you will not see,
nor the hooded Santa in the gown all white
and trimmed with blood. You would wake free

to clear my eyes, your body calm with sleep;
you, warmest, who were never much of a dream,
my arm around you.
                                        – Or nights you creep back round
to me, your hazy gown our scheming wraith.

My arm dragged in the dark across shroud white.
My blind-spot in our room. Oh love, what's wrong?
You left my bed so many nights, one night.
Be reasonable, love; no, not the white lace.
Wear the quilted black. And don't be long;
my arm lays only a little warmth in your place.

Clearing

After so long to fetch up with silver birch,
bracken inflating with the breeze, the dry
springy mat of needles, the mind's purchase,
where only homely ghosts retrace the by-ways.

That trunk, with all the torsion of a girl
elbowing her slip above her head, dead wish
or memory. (A life-long stepper-out, you were,
foot over silken splash with a cat's precision.)

No walks by still waters, hoping for seas,
nor where oaks writhe. These silver birch
will do; they always have, beyond all reason.
I shall not wander into you round here.
Winter is mine, the bare boughs emerging.
My ways have narrowed, these dry sticks my clearing.

Moth

A flake of wood, chip off the old block,
that's what you must be. And as for me,
I must be cracking up. Why otherwise
this inordinate affection for a moth,
the size of a fingernail? And on my clean
grey shirt. D'you think it's elm or pine?
D'you too seek refuge from the local woods?
The rust corrupts here. Tell me, what's the pull?

Flit. To the skirting-board. Why home on me?
Find yourself some bare and natural wood.
I won't clean too hard. I don't want to kill you.
Stay solo. More of you will pull the wool
over my eyes that way. No, out of that beam!
– Did she once wear a varnish of this colour?

Long Evenings

A patch of sun, you were, on the bare arm,
unnoticed by the mind in reading – warmth.
I read on in memory, for what it's worth,
to feel that sash of sun, and you not far.
The sunset moves around again. I stare
upon a page shone blank, till vision swims.
And long before, you would have come to whizz
the curtains to and shadow me and stay.

I turn the chair. A blade of iris spins
in a trill of its own local little winds.
Oh, love, I would have hastened up, long since,
to let you come and sit and see it twirl
from just this point of view. No, turn
your head a little more. No, as you were.

One Off

A cool glass, the long vista to the hill,
a girl, her shadow try-squared up the wall,
mirage of water on tarmac, glinting, still.
In the mind music I cannot quite recall.
And cherry-blossom daisied on the grass.
A sun-shaft turns the pages of the book.
As once you held my eye, I watch her pass,
and someone waiting draws her with his look.

The movement, not the mover . . . Oh, my love,
frivol of hesitation in the slow peal
of the skirt. (No, saffron yours, and blinding still.)
How many days that slight grace caught the life.
I could have buried all with that. . . . To pull
off the time of our life in unrepeatable style.

Memorial

Not this see-through stuff of memory. Rock,
that's what I need, granite. No more black lace
like winter saplings linked across the sky.
– This saffron blurring. – Something I can knock
the roughness off for years and yet still trace
your fine features; something I cannot ply
with drinks – a slim throat I cannot choke –
Your mountain-force of hair in the sun-smoke.

Above the eye-lash, single ply of cord!
Dove shadow in its curve; the arching brow –
who else saw that? Strong-backed as a fish leaps.
How clear it is, and clean out of the mind's hoard.
How real . . . love, is it you? Is it you now?
Let it be stone, love, where the flesh creeps.

Earthbound

Earth-flame, crocus under the ploughed bark,
earth-light, I have to kneel to look within.
Some peace, down here, horizon saucered, thin,
the children's noises scrambled through the park.
Half turn the head: blue sky without a mark
to move it by, though still that sense of spin.
Turn back, and let the mauving mist begin
before the sun makes everything go dark.

Earth-flame, earth-light – what kind of fool
would lay his head so close to rising fire,
so close to gnarling roots? Earth cool . . . earth cool!
Low mist on the sky-line, the chain-link wire.
So cool to touch, this bloom, a breath of air
stirring the steady flame to a small flare.

Window

Your eyes, child, in the window: the steady gaze
focused on nothing special, it would seem,
unless that chestnut in the day's last sun,
as though you wouldn't really dream of it
yet liked to think the candles' inner mist
would light the coming dark. Something of her
in that, her hidden self a wistful look.
More human yours and yet you stir dead love.

Reflections cross the pane but not your face,
and mine will never touch you as they pass;
my gangling matchstick man a trace of sun
no more to you across the grass. Yet, child,
your soft focus already blends out hers –
my love, you make the darkness personal.

From *Too Much of Water*

Dedication

For you who waste no speech
    to pass the light of day
    contented with your mute
flowers, the natural pleach
    of boughs, I drop these lines.
Look, earth-spots in the snow
    where every grass-blade leans.

Last Wishes

Love, sleep, and do not see me edge away.
    I cannot watch beside your death-bed.
Turn your head towards the close of day.
    I know the madness that is in your method.

How you will want the snowy impermanence of ash,
    your dust, like grass-seed, flighted over heath-land,
drifting in spinneys where the boughs clash,
    with matted needles laying waste beneath them.

Ah, settle on some narrower plot, beloved,
    among the blond spent grass and lie there;
not in the rain, nor in the wind ungoverned.
    Love, I cannot mourn you everywhere.

Last Words

All is as you have heard;
no, not asphodels,
not a gibbering word.

So you must think of rain;
on spring's first daffodils
I'll fall for you again.

But not for some years.
Last April's dust is laid
under a hollow lid.
And who is in these tears?

Spring

Yes, yes, we watched so many things die;
    lamented the fresh green of the willow
and sundry roses under this or that sky –
    and much else mourned into a pillow.

We knew full well it came to this.
    So I offer you this nostalgia of grief,
and these sprigs of forsythia, not much amiss,
    that blossom before they come to leaf.

Interflora

Ah, flowers . . . that said as much as your quick nudge
to snap a bee reversing, all velour;
your walks to calibrate a book of hours
with bud-shut of your wild ones – all to scrap
your wristwatch half a year. I'll tell you flowers:
crocus slopped open like a pair of scissors
beyond the point of closing in the fist.
In my mind's eye they inscribe their locus.

And since I cannot talk to you alive
I'll speak to you as dead, say it with flowers.
(More beauty in their day than in our life.)
They'll thrive, perfection's clones; nothing to me,
they'll pierce you with my nothingness – bleak
mauve footlings which you cannot pick and choose.

By-way

It's baffling, every time I pass, this shifty sense
that you had known the place, that we were intimates
of something here: a path; this now vestigial
track; which wildflower clump? what leafy fugitive
whose glimpse we'd make our own? But nothing tangible.

What is this? The lane is gone wherever it goes.
Never much of a one in my experience
for walks or views, why play the local genius
of diminutions? We never were unanimous;
what chance you'd keep omniscience to a picnic spot?

– I get you echoing, your voice a little wearier:
'Moments we had, the days, the days are vanishing.'

Look there! Lady's-slippers. Will they satisfy?
Let them. I'll track them down again. I promise you.

Rendezvous

You know: the old pear-tree stood
beside the hazel. The evening gleam
hatched to silver the leaden stream.
You will remember that spot
(I have taken pains you should)
whether you will or not,
with the coxcombs that you pull
from the cobnuts in the fall.
(Come back, Peter; come back, Paul.)

Where it used to shrink or fill
only a row of hazel sprigs.
And it dried out in my time.
– The name of that bourn is Styx,
poor, bare, forked, divining stem.

Clusters

That many must have loved in this grey world
much as we have is some companionship
as once again I trace the languid sweep
your brow-bone shapes, wing of a frigate bird.

I tell myself that I can love the years
that fanfold from the corner of your eyes,
your laughter; more, how I alone can phase
the shadowed hint of dove your lids curve clear.

Even the galaxies cluster deep in space;
infinitudes of planets where we lie
again together linked in love or sleep.
– Ah, my love, it's unbearable society.
Even this desperation, that steers my hand
to grip you, grips you also in the stars.

Moment

If you could know how much I train myself
against that moment you would understand
my quiet anger at your breakneck paths,
your bare legs angled in the sun like fish;
my vacant gaze on you patient in the flowers,
hidden in sprays of bright forsythia,
the stems unseen, your time-drift galaxy.
In so much green to gloss the turn of day!

And you might gather then, even in dream,
how in my restlessness I turn to you
and touch that lath of muscle by your ear
and stir a tress because I cannot bear
to watch you sleep away when I have thought
to keep all for myself the darkest night.

The Brooch

It's not so much the amber stone.
  I don't think any follow quite,
but you perhaps will get the gist:
  I bought this filigree on sight
because it seemed to catch the tone
  of silver birch in silver mist.

The gift, not giving, is the gist;
  but why I love that tone in tone
I can't get clear, nor really quite
  why you should ever like the sight
of silver birch more than the stone.
  You'll please me if you wear the mist.

Over that rise we'll find low mist
  and find the birch but not your stone.
Come from behind me, hand in glove.
  Primeval instincts still persist:
I almost turned on you. Oh love,
  the cracking twig bred in the bone.

Path

Now we have come to this. Take a long look.
After the years, the wandering, this the return:
the landscape, if you say, of childhood. – Fern,
we couldn't see beyond it. Never that brook
you try unravelling to the sky's scuffed brink,
the caterpillar hedgerows wandering far.

This path, and beechnuts we were hunting for.
Our matchstick shadows buckled down and shrank.

I cannot bring myself to shuck them now;
I feel the tricorne husk lifting the nail.
But we'll be back and often now you know. –
Beechnuts. My stylish love, you'd have to kneel.
Listen, grasshoppers chirring in the quitch
like the spasmodic winding of a watch.

Wall

Oh not again. Two hundred miles from home
the tile-topped wall, pointed with angled moss,
an ancient puddle in the rutted loam,
fly-wings of oil. And was it? Yes, it was,
loosestrife. – A moment seen those years ago
one everlasting country afternoon.
Ah, now the dust and heat and thirst of June,
and, worse, an echo of that wretched hope:

that there would be in time a postern gate,
and gnats, loyal as these eye-motes, gone;
and we should come upon a shaded lawn,
not as expected guests or the long lost
but visitants of joy, and glimpse at last
the past intrinsic flit like a rabbit's scut.

Exorcism

You're boning up on me again. The years
I've waited! Hardly. More like stopped and paused
in odd moments, hearing some phrase once yours,
for you to sidle up – and dither-paced
as usual. I know. I know all your shifts:
limp jokes – you couldn't stand a decent silence;
fidgets you took for action or resilience;
fake laughter turning jester all my shafts.

You never had the nerve to lie quite straight.
Palters and shifts. Now it all must wait.
Or can you fidget up some haze all white;
or shall I come to get you? Fat chance, it seems.
You're getting warm. Warmer. . . . Only in dreams
the living haunt the dead in their long night.

Gifts

Upon the flyleaf your dearest name
    and: 'Happy Christmas, Nineteen Eighty';
    a book you'll toss aside so lightly,
thinking it dull, as may be I am.

One day you'll read and love this volume,
    as well I knew when I inscribed,
    and, seeing the diminutive script,
you'll wish perhaps it were on vellum.

And bridge to these old days behind
    as once I did, discarding a hymnal
    and catching in it like a hangnail,
on the endpaper my father's hand.

Against Superstition

FOR DONALD DAVIE

Most vows sworn in youth long broken;
attrition of years yawns rightly so;
but one sworn deep and never spoken,
made to myself those rigid years ago.

Never to write a congratulatory line,
never to fellow maker speak in verse,
for to speak so would twice assign
the poet's title – from all but Death a curse.

Thus, as Landor, who is safely dead,
I now address you, in this guise
risking Death's silence on my head,
and you who taught me much say is it wise?

Winters

IN MEMORIAM YVOR WINTERS

Because you knew how all earth's furies
    could leak through candle-flame into a room
you latched on reason's mail against the lurid
    and caught the light but not the gloom.

And since you thought the evil of the curse
    could only be removed by words that wove
no spell by feeling's fluke or mind's inertia,
    proof in themselves though in the sacred grove,

I shape these words, the almost foreign parlance
    we both imagine ours as born and bred,
and weave your myth of reason against all jargons,
    here in this study lit by nuclear dread.

Birds

FOR KEVIN CROSSLEY-HOLLAND

Not the opinions and propositions of Livy,
Cicero's studied rhetoric, Virgil's stately rhythms –
this dead lingo of squared stones, more gaudy and more
lively,
naive flowers and gawky birds, the dolphin-rider's,
in frieze and mosaic, uncluttered and lovely.

Full sun helps to envisage them, lax on their hillside –
none of the Lachrimae Christi, more proto-Frascati.
Never before inveigled by sun, I people the whole scene,
envy their space, this same light with the high cloud
scudding,
though they stroll in my head as I sit on the hall seat.

Yet my flier is none of their stiff-legged, perky songsters;
no, nor car-crushed sparrows killed in their hedge-hopping:
the lone hawk that held its glide through the gable's sawn
trees,
down the banquet-hall, above the mead and the harping,
out into darkness with the smoke ascending.

Fishbourne

An Apology

FOR ROBERT LOWELL

A touch of jealousy, good shade,
it must have been when I deplored
the second thoughts you spread abroad,
your chance to change what you had made.

The printed phrase you could re-word
in answer to the wayward muse;
so let the rashness of my views
be never seen again or heard.

Considered long, too late expressed,
I breathe this brief apology
and covet with keener jealousy
your incommunicado rest.

The pathless search that hoodwinked you
has led me through the mud and mire
where all that comes of mortal fire
is jack o' lanterns half seen through.

Rest, rest, immortal spirit, rest
upon your laurels once again
and leave me to the itching pen
where straight deletion's much the best.

Summer Shadows

That toddler, hoicking his shadow bootee up the step,
like someone who has stuck his foot in tar,
will make in later time a summer of this spell.
    His mother, laughing at the top,
her hair in tints of copper beech may store
for someone summer in a lock that will not pale.
I watch the road-stone in the tarmac form and speed
like comets through my shadow, raise my pace
    to see them hasten – which has spurred
a boy with whirr of tyres to race and pass.
Quicksilver threads, light vacillates along each spoke.
    And there beyond the brow expands
        in my mind, at least,
after the tunnel of trees, like green arrested smoke,
the everlasting sea on ever lengthening sands.
        Cease! Ceased.

Ah, woman, child, and man and boy, unknown confreres,
your shadows, briefer than a roadside rose,
hold still, imprinted as one summer's phase,
    glossed forms through which no stone careers.
No chiaroscuro of leaves obscure this frieze.
Loved silhouettes, whose darkness time intensifies,
I'd give you names; I'd conjure namesakes with your image,
and times to come recall this choice of summers
    fading to the future's, homage
of eyes that look upon these gleams and shimmers.
Yet, if they come to love them, no second sight,
    but poignant with what's dead and done –
        as in their day.
Ah, love, you're somewhere in this summer's light,
walking the wildflower paths, out of the sun,
        away, away.

Contingencies I'd fix in frescoes made of slate.
Shadows of flame cast out by greater light,
I cannot let you go where all the leaves are strewn,
    a summer sepia obsolete.
I'd give you by some quirk or sleight
indelible salience. – First drops of rain
tacked into the pavement, that avenue
of flowering cherry's earliest pinkest snows –
    Cobham. . . . It's all together now.
Once, once, but where I can no longer recognize. . . .
Unknown comrades, I've spoken for your sakes and mine.
    In asphalt pavements, a decor of flakes.
        But what will hold
together is a redolence returning, touched with brine. . . .
Love, comb, comb out the rain-fresh scent of woods and
brakes. . . .
        The shades turn cold.

From *Earth Light*

Portents

Strangest things have happened before,
    again, and mostly elsewhere:
sparrows will nest in a tractor – folklore
    the runes of geese on the air.

And our recounting them as rare
    bandies their wonder back to us . . .
and if the thrush we see is a fieldfare
    is the marvellous instance bogus?

And if, love, we both speak at once
    in the light of some other summer,
and say it is love, in all conscience,
    it has happened again somewhere.

Our shadows link hands in the wildflowers,
    gangling their length on the pathway,
and that chink-chink we hear as ours
    lights only once on this twayblade.

Cranesbill

Delicate misty bloom
    huddled away like your words,
a cranesbill of powdery blue,
    mute for all its worth;

not to be gathered or pressed
    where it may grow again.
Let it grow here for the present
    we never took nor gave.

Gifts

The thoughts I have I cannot give.
I hardly bear them well myself.
Gifts of my hands I'd like to give
and tell we share them here and now.

What the gift gives is what I'd give –
Behind this dumb, so yellow bloom.
I'd like to give you happiness,
the cat that seldom comes when called.

Occasions

I wasn't there to look
    the time you saw the lightning sear
the crooked oak.
    I had your fear for it.

I wasn't there the day
    you found a wind-cast blossom-shadow
spread from the may.
    Your joy I had for that.

– You let the bird go free.
    I couldn't see the hope that welled
but it seemed to me
    a bulb you held had bloomed.

When the love that I swear
    is a dry husk on the wind's breath,
I shan't be there.
    You'll have my death for it.

Memento

What is this, you can't remember?
You have it pat if I forget.
You gave your word. The sun was amber,
setting. You know, by that gate.

So low it silvered drops of rain
beneath the bars. You reached your right
hand out to them, your fingers ran
them through and cross-marked the straight.

It's unbearable you can't remember.
The world's tears, woman. I was there.
That cliff of cloud, bruise-black and sombre
above the sunset's orange shore.

Some game! Forget the promise, love.
Recall the place that you swore on.
Yes, circumstantial – known as life.
We cannot go back there again.

Trapezoid shadow of the gate –
We used to try to change each other.
I can't believe that you'd forget.
When was it that we gave it over?

Antique

A silver candelabra, love?
Why on earth a candelabra?
Silver? Never in your life.

Or is it the olden days you're after:
a bit of tallow in an old tin?
Which of whose forebears lit a castle?

The twisted stems at every turn
reflect a tilted flame of lamp-light –
a marriage of convenience, and tone.

But we can never light those candles;
nor wander back to last spring, even.
You leapt from my grasp, darted to paddle

your hands in the bluebells' haze, and the life
came back to you in that wild laughter,
at finding a pool the storm had left.

I've waited for you in the thick of darkness,
well-shaft to a pitch lid of water,
my head obstructing the only star-point.

Do not come back, my bluebell wader,
do not pull back from your dwindling pool.
Once in living memory your wood.

Look, I have lit the candles. They pile
our quaking shadows over us.
Watch them. Watch as their tears spill.

Goldenrod

More is forgotten than remembered.
    I cannot tell you why it is I hate
    these goldenrod. I've always hated them,
and any goldenrod, by any gateway.
    One day when I am old and the glossed light
    of childhood seems eternity too late,
it may come back to me in living spite,
    prompting some feeling for an hour or spasm –
    dull, yellow-dusted peaks of even height –
when, deaf to me, the feigned enthusiasm
    of your vague words that never had a season
    is painless as passing time, the trembling aspen;
and love's become as trivial as these
    stalks of goldenrod, well out of it,
    that I smash and enjoy smashing as I please
because they have their season, and they split
    cleanly, unlike the pliancy of trees.
– Now match your forceful mouth to this mad fit.

Bric-à-Brac

The glance of years ago,
    one forgotten afternoon,
you cannot now return, eyes slow,
    the gaze immune.

Okay, look around the room,
    old gifts, odd curios shelved;
silent, uninvolved, presume –
    your years undelved.

Clairvoyant to my days,
    you have the vantage over me.
Date my ivory, appraise
    this fake in memory:

a naked figurine, its style
    wide open, one for a pair,
Chelsea blue period, trial
    piece, none too rare.

Come in, do; and ring the bell,
    eyes immune, slow as that swan
in all-time junk. Pawn and sell,
    the antique con.

LIKE A VOW

A Sequence

Local Colour

It feels like farewell to leave this area,
as if to go would lose some thing of value,
though what it is I have no clear idea.

Not those cool harmonies, ochre and blue,
these hessians, barley golds, the rusting bracken,
the Autumn scorches in the fields of fescue.

That pathway like a single wheel-rut, then;
redolent of somewhere that it wanders,
some journey long to rest, some friend forgotten?

No . . . nor the angled bough whose shadow stirs
some element of dream across the moment.
Nothing to do with you, my love, nor others.

It holds no aura of a lost event,
mine or the land's; no calm of mind; no trespass;
nor is there terror in it like a portent.

It's almost love that holds me to this space –
despite a world I thought to leave at will –
in dread its power may rise in other places.

Recapitulation

A blade of cold water down the throat:
huddle of trees and shrubs like green sheep;
the mill-pond brimming still as lead with threat.

And, if, with these unsummoned into shape,
they all are there, and bound up with my head,
all days are there to rise with detail sharp,

can't I riffle to whichever day I had,
and won't one show me what it is I want –
untouchable, exact, and facet-hard,

as once I stared myself into a squint
to catch, in the spouting barley-sugar-amber,
the skelter of the tea-leaves as they went?

Nothing. But in the cup the usual number,
dregs, always dregs – though grandmother at least
made fortunes of them, as I now remember

one distant day when I was fearfully lost –
wrong fork across the heath, not seen ahead,
when coming from her cottage – time now glassed,

untouchable, enacted, period.
And what the child would not, cannot know:
speedwell, red campion, in all likelihood.

– So many lanes they way-mark and renew
that lead to nothing much that I would find:
speedwell, red campion, ragwort, I name them now.

They intervene, again have intervened,
but those days passed as weeds some mood or itch
idly dispersed, or swinging jacket fanned.

Day! Where is the day I did not watch
hands move, mind churn – its laughter free or feigned?
Merciless eye, that nothing can assuage.

Upland

I

A dry ditch, with banks of leaf-mould
like wet rust, chestnuts overhanging;
a slate sky, contoured with sun-gold

above the horizon where a hamlet
glistens. There will be rain, rain falling
big and warm and straight as a plummet,

splashing up coronets. . . . Forgotten
the hamlet's name, the last turning,
which next, but southern the location.

But I was on that upland; remember
a pressure binding and releasing.
My memory haunts it like a spectre.

Perhaps it is the mind of others
that leaguer there almost a feeling.
– You would assume the wild-eyed watchers.

I find you many likely places.
But, if you're there, you show no inkling.
You give them all your keenest glances,

then off into the woods to savour
the bluebells' well attested pooling –
lady's-slippers found one summer.

But what is missing I cannot capture
in trees, lane, ditch, the cloud purpling.
It is nothing that is in your nature.

But I am nearest it in silence:
the sound of a bell no longer ringing.
It's almost like an old allegiance,

fealty sworn young to a lost lord.
You cannot swear faith to my ghost-king.
I cannot breach his word, his gold-hoard.

Your bluebells, lass, this is your kingdom.
In my lord's realm I'm the hireling.
Kneel to the bluebells, the blown blossom.

No once and future king, fore-spoken:
his line will never see returning.
My oath can never be forsaken.

2

Lord, in the under-light of thunder –
But if my liege is self-projection,
no ghostly exile of a lost order,

loyalty is no less, though kingship
is mine. What worse than king's treason?
I can't break faith by cant or gossip.

I say: no feint of trees and shadow.
Not mine but earthly the dominion;
the bond is real as voice and echo.

No: beeches these; the promised shower
small rain; and the wide sky ocean-
grey, not true to scarp and tenor.

But let it be: a part and parcel,
our common ground of recollection,
the great, down-sweeping branches focal.

(Curled husks of nuts like Dutch bonnets,
the short-cut – geese in opposition,
a slate sky harrying high cloudlets.

We used to eat the nuts when children,
nails lifted by the shell's construction. . . .)
Childhood, and the big rain not fallen.

3

Coronets of rain – and the keen-eyed
child recalls their brief existence,
sprung from the tarmac of the roadside.

And, going up the narrow staircase,
Candleman prancing like a nuisance,
coronets, tumbled in a goose-chase,

rolling down the gleaming rooftops.
In the stillness of leaves and birds, the silence,
the weathered spirit senses raindrops,

knows the freshness that falls, releasing
the tension, bringing out the fragrance
of the grass, the dry ditch jingling.

– Trembler of light on its white column,
coronets tumbling, dancing attendance,
Candleman, Candleman, once his kingdom.

But to your beeches as I know them,
my scarp, how shall we plot our credence?
To know another takes a kingdom.

And the big rain is falling, watcher,
the big drops in their regular cadence,
bigger than any tears, and warmer.

The Sunken Path

A land it was without companion.
No feature to detain the eye,
no sign of human cultivation.

I do not know how many times
I'd been there; have no recollection
of what event, nor where or why.

And yet it will not be forgotten:
the grass banks burred first left, then right,
like hammered pegs, the path so sunken.

Those weird birches, trunks awry,
the course that raindrops latch on
down a dirty pane – and the pines,

encroaching pines at the edge of vision.
The path wound up a steepish climb,
toward a slate sky without motion.

– Years ago, years, the lingering sight,
but clearer, sharper the depiction.
It seems to lock into the mind.

*

But what holds over the hill-crest?
Do the pines' serrations meet
like jaws – a dark aquarial forest?

Was shelter once the driving need,
from bead-curtains of rain – or coolest
shade from the dusty August heat?

The path draws upward, still the clearest.
If you'd been walking there with me,
there would be something you had noticed,

a skipper, wildflower prove it real.
Your eye for small things always honest
to pin locality on a dream.

Show me the colour of bugloss, dearest;
fix it as somewhere you have been,
you with your eye for a wren's nest.

*

But which and where are the companions?
Are they long-barrowed by the tread;
this the landscape of extinctions?

– In mind, I climb the likely bed
of winter rills, and the desertions
grow as congenial as a friend.

The path holds no commemorations.
Nor were you one to reach the head.
The air trembles with the derelictions.

There should be, just beyond the crest,
a church of leaning headstones, apparitions
of other people's, not my dead,

living times out of mind, deletions
of lichen, moss, the rain's fret;
but I, too, have made my exactions.

I have buried them before their death;
the living shall not haunt their perditions.
Love, the landscape seeps into my head.

*

– The boy stares long into the window,
watching a raindrop dither downward,
seeing another and another follow.

They're lit to silver at an awkward
juncture, to silver birch; the narrow
path meandering, pine bordered.

– Wenceslas footsteps, huge and hollow,
stilting the loose sand, striding upward;
those crumbling edges of sand-grains harrow

with the erratic stealth of rivered
drops on the pane that make an ox-bow
but always edging, inching earthward.

– The horror of bubbles on the cocoa
bursting, the dry grains uncovered,
imprinting memory like a furrow.

*

Where are the friends of this madness?
Banish me from the lie of this land.
Love, show me the colour of bugloss.

Gesture

Sand not discernible from sea,
the sea not separable from sky,
mist like eroding promontory.

A girl zigzags the shingle, striding
that drives her flaring yellow skirt
against her thighs, like flame plying

from underneath a bough; exertion
flapping her blonde hair from her shoulders –
a gale of her own with each diversion,

veering till mist obscures, then strolling
clear a moment. She has no plan,
no firm direction that is holding.

– Blurring the foreland, rifted in canyons,
encroaching combers that churn the stones –
mist and sea are her companions.

*

That self-wind, mine. She plays the loner:
hair and skirt, haphazard walk,
her pleasure in themselves, and donor

of mine, the emblems of a haughty
sorrow, germane to mist and headland,
consoled by sea, the wave's exhaustion.

And to the life. It is the death
of hope. (Long live hope, the skirt knows;
long live hope, the blonde hair threshes.)

Pensive, perhaps, a child, she notes
the sand responding to her feet,
like skin beneath some grip or load.

And so it may be joy, the freedom
of lonely cove and lingering mist,
nonchalant gestures; none to read them.

*

Mist and darkness obscure the figure.
A year ago? The gestures bloom
in streets and crowds, indelible vigour;

on hoardings, film – a casual beauty
or routine, but as the leaf runs true,
sorrow or joy, allusion, illusion.

Six feet of light between us, and soon the
dark. I want to reach my hand
to touch your hand. It is the movement

of twenty years ago, this angle,
wandering like a stopped clock in time.
Love? It is the gesture. The candle

has not changed its spear of light;
my gnarled hand knows its root and branch.
A thousand shearwaters, one dive.

The Hill

IN MEMORIAM R. C. GRAY

I cannot do anything with this landscape,
while you have settled down to see the views,
and gaze across the valley to some mansion

sinking in green suds of trees – amusement
enlivened for a moment by a train,
scaled to a model, that you find a nuisance.

I'd rather have it animate the ancient
peace, I suppose it is, of field and covert;
but no hand will descend on it – extraneous –

and shift it to some tunnel. I have no love
of miniatures, no god's yen for omniscience.
The aftermath is cut and stacked and covered.

And the path leads to stepping-stones; listen:
the sluice of water that is water. Tears
would sound the same in volumes such as this.

There is no voice in the stream's whispered hearsay.
There is no beauty here. It's all my eye.
See with the moth's light; catch the talon's fierceness.

Our tread erodes the path like the rain lying
on the sun's scorched earth; soft or wild, the rain
that I'm attuned to more than any shining

of the sun – rain never visited with angels.
And I remember once a day of downpours
when Bob, my friend – dead in his strength of brain-stroke,

spread one oilskin upon the grass and, pounded
by thunderous drops, both huddled, makeshift-tented
under the other cape against the trouncing.

We had a grass-furred oilskin when it ended,
and months before we'd plucked each blade or strand;
a talking point for years, our launching sentence.

My eyes are locked through rain into this landscape,
the stream and stepping-stones, the lucid shallows,
for my dead friend, and all of those whose handwork

is buried in each feature of the valley.
Love, you shouldn't see it from this angle.

Hold still. A leaf's caught in your hair. Mallow?

River

To hold in mind
these twisting paths,
this peace like the river winding.

How long will either keep
unblurred such peace
to flow on, sinewed, leaping?

That wren to be your emblem,
its jiffy poise,
pole-vaulter bending its stem?

Or these few speedwell mine
to make us pause,
return the river's winding?

But years, in distant years,
this time of peace
a drifting branch of hearsay?

That wren toppling a stem,
the speedwells' place?
Or like a vow remembered?

* * *

The Water-Splash

The water-splash, you called it,
typical understatement.
A long time since I saw it.

But still in mind located
and you still on the high-point,
gazing long to savour it.

Dumb appreciation. Silence. ...
We knew we'd change, and thought
this, too, would be sanitized.

Our focal waterfall,
like an old English sheepdog
lolloping nowhere forwards.

He has no name or meaning,
but I have sent you this dog,
summers, as if you'd see it.

No telepathic responses;
your clear eye unflummoxed:
water and stone and mosses.

You and the falls a comfort,
while I have lost the place,
imagined every summer.

And on a heat-hazed day
I picture you on the slope,
and see the dog again.

Fetch him, boy! Fetch him home!
(Shoo him off and dismiss him
or you'll be soaked all over.)

I can't understand this distance.
How was it less than your death?
I'm not used to the difference.

And back comes old tousle-head
every summer into mind;
and the water-splash, as you had it.

Still

Daughter, you are – if a photograph
    may tell the truth without the eyes
    touching in shady velleities –
your grandmother's image and proof.

As was your mother – with the same if.
    From those old days: the untrammelled gaze;
    such carefreeness that never goes;
the lace but useless handkerchief.

– Speedwell after speedwell, path
    or hedge to tell each by her place
    and time, the trellises, the plush,
a future like a picnic heath.

It's more than mood, the hasty comb,
    blouse loose, unceremonious.
    I cannot swear to carefreeness,
but hope you may, in time to come.

Not as a grey nostalgiast
    but knowing what had been yourself.
    – Lass, must the held frame dissolve?
Both hold the present in the past?

Speed well, my only lass, speed well.

Correspondences

FOR WALLY KAUFMAN

Letters as frequent as English rain,
    you have kept faith for twenty years,
    and faithfully that face appears
in mind, that shock of hair like grain
        before the scythe.

Don't tell me: you made the pub seethe
    hearing your plot to roast a swan.
    I now expect that marathon,
your six-mile trek in the blizzard's teeth
        to meet – by air.

Leaves under the closed door are
    lost voices in a foreign tongue.
    We scuffed them all about when young.
I've swept them up each year so far
        without fail.

Fall or Autumn, Autumn and Fall.
    And these rose-petals I gather
    make a wine that will not travel,
a scent and flavour I cannot file
    like an old address.

File this then in your legendries:
this photo of a grey-haired idler
(that doesn't really travel, either)
daydreaming into the autumn trees,
willows and wyches.

And what you cannot see he watches:
indolent swans on quiet waters,
cupping, like hands, wings poised and faultless
to catch the light; and his half-wishes
for that candid white.

Communication

FOR IAN HAMILTON

Now miles and years have intervened,
do you, as I do yours, old friend,
still read my books? Would either read
them more if one of us were dead?
And would a voice unearthed recall
the years of silence that appal?

Souvenir

The very earth on which they stood
is gone, three fists of withes,
poor pollards tilted at the wood's edge,
reeds like scythes upended, crossed.

Beneath cloud slabbed with storm,
    their image skimmed with light.
Far friend, I hope with you a faded torment.
    Hindsight seems the last betrayal.

The Line

FOR JULES LAFORGUE. INTER ALIOS.

Leaves rim the shores of lakes.
– We confirm your instances,
nodding acquaintances,
old friends, with knowing looks.

Tortoise-shell shuts its blazon,
and gnomon-like it dozes;
across the lawn the daisies
succeed the cherry-blossom.

Your words have changed no tone.
Spine gold gone from the row;
gold dust in the slant ray,
and summer on the turn.

The soft riffling of leaves;
owl's hoot on the bare field,
black place-mark in the fold,
the flicking of our lives.

Old friends, in the long shadows,
your cry goes through our head,
your cry goes through, still heard.
– Is it the lamp that shudders?

Life-Lines

Reading, in your hand, the searing care:
a lifelong friend insane, a child dead,
the bonds of love that tear, I catch the pain
in all you wrote and said.

I leech into your sorrow again – forgive me,
feeling through all I read in your slant black.
In the dead season I live, old friend, I need
even this to clutch me back.

Bookmark

FOR HUMPHREY CLUCAS

A musty book of fusty verse,
deciduous dust of the old school room.
Someone has pressed a shepherd's purse
that tints the page with winter bloom.

Enlivened, I, poor fool of time,
flick to the bookplate for a claim,
and wondering which had loved both rhyme
and flower, choose a faded name.

Steps

A woman speaks

Ah, let him count my footsteps down the street!
As if he could, this quiet night of snow.
But only these two feet go down the flags
and back again – wet pewter in the white.

I should have walked the unmarked roofs instead.
Daisies they look like, all those scrambled stars.
Soundlessly I tread; I'm like the snow.
This snow will never tell me who I am.

No tally of my footsteps in this hush.
Tonight, I'll pad up barefoot, soundlessly.
Back of a scrubbing brush, this dusty sole.
Strange with what narrowness we hold the ground.

A Woman Speaks to God the Father

Lord of the entire universe,
was there no one else to take?
No lively son in the womb's hearse,
no supple girl for you to break?

But you must take my dolphin man?
No boy to fall to you in play,
no white head broken like a fan,
no sinewed arm for you to fray?

Must I be jealous all my life
of six feet of claggy earth;
jealous of every trotting wife,
of every brat that's given birth?

I am jealous of you, God.
If I had every inch your might,
in my black hole you'd spoil your rod;
you'd kick up stars in endless night.

Memorial

IN MEMORIAM FRANCES HOROVITZ

I never met you.
    The gut reaction
to mourn your death is
    driven by anger
that time should wreck not
just you yourself but
anyone else so
    circled with love,
    gentle with life.

Nothing I miss is
    you or yours to
wrench recognition.
    I cannot mourn you.
I'd have to give you
characteristics,
a touch, some charisma
    of others I love to
    feel your destruction.

Helen's hands,
    cool even in summer –
the image happens
    with such a sudden
shudder of anguish
and terror I am so
cold that I cannot
    touch myself. My
    hands mourn your death.

MIRRORS, WINDOWS

A soliloquy: a middle-aged man observes his dead father's features in his reflection in the window pane.

A Likeness Reflects

Look at it, old face, in the window pane.
What do you think it feels? Thought you once knew:
timidity disguised beneath long patience;

weak humour an evasion playing neutral;
that everlasting hustle to escape
from any issue, household, local, nuclear?

– Tousled hairstyle, the voice's measured cadence,
those heavy spectacles . . . they hardly hide
the likeness. How have you come up to occasion?

But then it wasn't yours. (Who else with the hindsight?)
– You don't have to sit here and face this carping.
There you are, let that squirrel take the high-jump.

(Too many mirrors.) Spiral the trunk, scarper,
forelegs wide, back humped, a grand-prix car.

The Garden Beyond

A steady wind flows through the cherry tree;
along the topmost twigs aligns the leaves
like minnows swimming, motionless, upstream.

That low plank bridge across the bourn, a legion
of tiddlers holding station underneath;
those planks an ankle-width apart, unleashing

fears of legs in traps, a dread of kneeling
with all the rest. – Laughter without amnesty.
(Look away, face; true mirrors are amnesiac.)

Fear of water so deep it reaches to tears.
That inching down the face like insect duos.
– Dream of the leg bleeding ants, ants teeming.

Open the door. The rain will have to do
for this, child. Out. Out. Open the door.

Reflection Answers Back

The bone-house has no doors, and all the windows
reflect the images of self-defeat,
self-aggrandizement and self-acquittal.

Sit still. We'll flesh each other out, feature
for feature. Look on me, old man; as you used
to look; look on your son, feeling for feeling.

The long wait for triumph is over for you.
Not that gaze again, tacit and fixed.
You haunt weaker dead than living on my youth.

Silence consent? Or dumb déjà view? Fidget,
go on, give no answer. But do something.
Play with your pens, you've a whole fistful.

Old man, look on him; look on your son
with that shiftless iron stare, that air presumptive.

Reflection Rebukes and Challenges

There is a time for speech, a time for silence.
Death gives most men but you the sense of it.
There was a time for words; you did not desire them.

What the headstone speaks the living issue.
The dead shall not come to living beck and call.
You never heard me speak, not a single instance.

Ventriloquize me now from your little corner.
Speak to your son. (The pane stares back at you.)
Your son, not me. Time for the wise and cautious.

Ventriloquize me now! Here's to reunion!
And I shall tell if you talk in character.
I shall reflect on his and your ill-usage.

Ventriloquize me: muggins, the taciturn.
(Who says does not know. But you're determined.)

The Garden Beyond and Beyond

The minnow leaves have made no sign of headway,
flickering like light tethered in the current.
What water, sprats of sun, when Bob, quite helpless,

flashed skidding through the ford, one dry escutcheon
where saddle shielded trousers.
A sort of shining.
Like couch-grass-heads the gutter ripples scurry.

– The gold nib gleamed and buckled with my shying.
It was that day of grief my mother died.
I watch it crumple. Sorrow? Selfish icon,

my first fountain-pen, or true digraph?
Under the table with the torch-light dimming,
waiting for dark to hone the beam, motes diving

and soaring in the shaft. – I watch them dither,
drifting out into night. (Moth, you are dizzy.)

Wise and Cautious

Son, I cannot tell you how to live.
The lightning lasts a flashy second's worth.
Rock can't keep the spate inside its limits.

Oak cracks in storm; but mouths may keep their word.
I promise nothing; we shall miscomprehend
each other and possibly do much worse.

Yet do not look on this in long years hence
and blame yourself for every misconception,
nor grieve when I am gone upon this head.

Promise me nothing; vows are sworn to the self:
make sure the word you give will wear like diamond.
(And one other thing: get yourself an obsession.)

Son, I cannot tell you how to die.
So do not watch me. No date for your diary.

Reflection Heckles

That's not very knowing. What do you say?

My words are silent. Silence that is golden.
(Slaves of the crucified deserve the same

in image of the only (mis)begotten.
You couldn't manage that, so had to sham
self-martyrdom, all those petty golgothas.)

Not even the sun is enough. We are shadows
of flames and risk becoming the shadows of bombs.
Twice a day the brilliant sun can shackle

our hind-leg stance to its stalking bondage,
the squat tortoise at noon, the gangling hank
at sunset. We have parodied the body

of the dog, the cat, the horse, but never hatched
so many creatures fashioned without hands.

Colloquy

A handyman, is it, now? And what can hands
do more than minds about it? Pull the curtains?
Fidget with pens? Settle a tinker's haggle?

– Your hand, man, from the grave, and in my cursive
so studiously unlike yours, old bible ham;
give me your hand, conclude this running skirmish.

Give me your hand; you never gave me a hand.

– The dead can't plead for those that live and suffer;
the living may not pray for the dead. The has been
is forever has been. Advise your son
while he is still alive. Put him wise.
Feed experience to his wide presumption.

Trust you to put it straight in black and white.

– Or the old block will know the reason why.

He Addresses himself to Reflection

The minnow leaves have made no headway yet.
The only way is down, for all their darting,
and they, like you, go down without a yelp.

Father, father, no more; the glass is dark.
I've put the light out. Now the moths have gone.
You've never haunted darkness, poor cadaver.

You're laid to rest. I give my word as gospel.
I suppose I'll watch the leaves, the squirrel
a few more years, still heckle autumn's gossip,

sometimes catch your tones. I cannot acquit you.
And this abeyance gives no satisfaction.
Lie easy as ever – and forgive this quibble.

– Years, years spent pouring words we couldn't fathom.
Only through death we speak in honest fashion.

Ventriloquy

My son, you haunt me with my hasty youth.
The genes have won. And nothing I have tried
has saved you from the worst, or been much use.

You look at me as I have stared in triumph
over my father, seeing only what seemed
incomprehension, suffering his casual triteness.

I don't much like the glare of your conceit.
I've lived your mood. You haven't reached my mood
or feeling, history or hope, season for season.

If you look, there is a blue tinge to the moon.
Sliver of apple on the knife. – My voyage
is almost over; your promontory is moving.

Who's speaking, please? Father, is this your voice?
Late, so late. The line is dead. Void, void.

A Time to Speak

I wanted to say much more than this.
But at the time with all the talk
I couldn't think how best to speak.

The time of our life in front of us,
but I misjudged how long it took
weighing the moment I should pick.

You'd turn, I thought, towards me, torn
to utter that long-building cry
half gathered through your idioms.

I've been too quiet. You didn't turn,
but like a wild bird wintering came
to me . . . and I have given you crumbs.

– Is it a bearable snow? Don't leave.
Don't go. . . . This waiting has been love.

Outcry

The pain is within me, wordless.
Why should I cry out
and add it to the world's?

You neither, don't you speak,
and for the same reason.
Don't try a single scream.

If my hand were in your hair
we could short-circuit the world.
What a stroke that would be.

Platonic

You never raped my soul – and that is why
I hate you. Everything you thought you'd had:
my little finger, lips, my barefoot pad,
tilt of the head, fishnet across a thigh,
as if these held in truth the very thing.
And the old burrow to the familiar dark,
your knick-knack cyclotron to hold that spark
in vacuo by conjuring in the ring.

Your soul, poor stump, has never made my soul.
But mine would soon have shown you what rape is,
if you were of my kind, near my black hole.
– Dream easier to chase, death easier to lay,
than going round this corner where I turn away.
this birch I touch into your memories.

Parting Gift

This is my last and lasting gift to you:
a locket. Empty, and empty will remain.
I bind you here with all the force I can raise:
give it the next hapless, willowy goof
to shack up with you.
– This you'll never do.
First, it's too complicated to explain;
best, your last chance to cross me all your days.
Go on. Right now. Fling it over the roof.

Not something to remember till you die,
my planted bug. You'll not forget: you ditch
the damn thing, hide, or give it. She's to try
to keep or junk it. You'll remember this bitch.
A locket. Empty. A singularity,
black voidlet that will waste you. Only me!

World Tour

Wherever you shall go, whatever do,
I shall be there. Just wait. Shut all the doors.
Yes, yes. I know it physically can't be true.
And mind, I'd never hang about in yours.
And as for metaphor, I've lost you there.
And you would think I'd have at least to die,
to die and, desiccated into air,
blow all about the world to catch your eye.

But you forget the language. Try foreign parts.
I'll mark some words with me, my direct line,
dearest, till death . . . you lie with. I'll spring on you
like guilt from words you seldom used or knew,
forgive me. And daily shock you with your arts
and crafts, your sniping hatreds. Vengeance is mine.

Journey

Dearest, I've gone at your pace.
We've lingered on the way;
some route you chose to trace.
It's taken us all day.

Let's have some give and take.
You've named the flowers. Look sharp.
It's not so far to make.
I'm going down that scarp.

That way we're there by dark.
Ah no, don't name the stars!
Sidereal meadow-spark?
Well, not all the stars.

Autumn Colour

How you laugh each year to watch the sparrows
flying in, and almost hidden, filching
berries from the firethorn. You can spare them.

That low laugh is why I like their fling,
wondering how the little buggers miss
impalement on the barbs a good inch long.

Some of them have stripped the elder tree.
You'd planted that for two good sorts of wine.
We wonder which prefer it or if all try.

How many other women used to love
watching through time these sparrows dart and hide
to steal their better thoughts and give a laugh.

You planted it for autumn colour once,
now for the birds in winter – part of our life.
And that low laugh, one of my seasonal wants.

You'd have planted it for all those women,
if you had ever known them, anticipating
your life and mine.
                                        The birds are almost human,
shaking their beaks like fingers stuck to paper.

Monologue

Years? It seems an aeon
that I have kept faith,
whatever that might mean
without volition or oath.
You left me little option –
Your talents, your serial spleens.
Always the exception,
you with your fine lines.

But I know what it means
in slither, self-disgust,
and icy blue moons.
Not that you'd have guessed.
Fat chance you're flesh and blood.
The last far pane of light
has flicked down like a lid.
The night is absolute.

– But isn't there some plane,
abstract, where the stars arch,
or at least Himalayan,
where this would count for much,
some brilliant white space?
And might this plane be yours?
Where we'd come to the odd pass
to tally the dead years?

– I cannot stop the mind
throwing you up again,
in its world without end,
neither has been nor bygone.
Shall we ever break even?
What torture in my mind
your twists and turns have woven.
This hell I recommend.

Bequest

Your rear-view mirror on to happiness –
you used to call it that if ever asked:
the scene is anywhere, too picturesque.
A stream meanders, glinting; two paths
meet at a bridge symmetrically, repeat
odd patterns from the winding of the stream.

A keepsake of you? You knew there was no need.
How could a meagre bit of earth dismiss
what years and miles had never done? The scene,
the long cherishing, is your farewell gift.
As you'd have wished, it hangs now on my wall –
the distance fringed with pines where I would walk.

But what you saw and treasured on that bridge,
or who you met there then – or down which path –
and where you stood to want this view of it
I cannot bring to mind on your behalf.
What you have cherished here I can't possess.
The two paths merge your absence into death.

3

From *Under the Breath* (2002)

Answer

Oh, slowly answer, my phlegmatical,
from what you do in your unruly flowers;
with that sense of timing, always yours,
avert the angry impatience of a second call.

The hours I've watched and hardly could endure
because I want something back – yes, still;
anything, without the way you stall.
Listen, my earth-bound love, I'm calling you.

I listen out with all the old impatience,
and you've long known exactly how I'm fixed,
but take your time again – and mine – unfussed.
Slowcoach, I live again with the old passion.

This dumb fury is all that's left to love.
Forgive me, forgive me – as if you are alive.

Visitation

So cool, this moss;
cool even as your hands were, always,
even in your raving.

I have laid you living
and, in this cold, cold place,
I would lay you dead –

if my spirit,
as never once in life,
could touch your spirit,

and one of us,
voiceless, could whisper
the word, peace.

Nocturne

This is a day like any of the days
the years have sidled past like so much else
and yet I do not want this one to close.

Leaves on the cherry-tree are turning black
in sprays up from the base. The darkness fills
and rises like the water in a lock.

Buff cloud that sidewinder ebbs have signed
goes smoothing under; the tide is still so low
it can't be told from twilit sky or sand.

– Shore where I'm waiting for a distant cry
that calls me to, from where I do not know:
from sea; the beach; the high-lit cliff or scree.

This dateless day is inching to an end.
I cannot summon a cry, as child I could,
nor hold the light up longer in my mind.

So other days will wane where I must wait,
nor welcome darkness as I mostly would,
but keep the mind alert for that cry in quiet.

Or echo of a cry I should have heard.
They say the dead do not appear in dream
but can they speak from far off, can they hide?

She did not cry between onset of dark
and day that night I listen in the dim
of dusk, of dawn, when ghost and living walk.

Lullaby

A woman speaks

To another country you've been taken.
How soundly do you sleep?
What language must you learn on waking?
I don't know when you weep.

My old, suede-soft, homely darkness
was lit by your piercing scream.
Last night, did you look on a different starscape
when I cradled you in dream?

No Visitors Beyond this Point

FOR K. D. 1967

Head bowed but that walk still cocky
you climb back up the rise.
And watching that walk from boyhood
I pick you out at once in the crowd
and know the verdict.

No need for words.
Your tears draw stares across the muddy car-park.

I'd take your arm
and guide you, tear-blind,
toward some more secluded place
but know you'd shake me off
as I would you.
I edge round
to block the gawpers out.

You sniff and grin,
heave out in sobs:
'You always had the luck,
you bastard, you.'

What is my sympathy?
You want my son.

For Keith

IN MEMORIAM

Brother, I lay this wreath upon the bier,
thwarted in grief that when this rite fell due
I thought you'd be the one to place it here
over a brother still as dear as you.

Coastwise

FOR PIERS

We walked by rivers, dreaming of seas.
On scarps we'd peered for other lands;
pitied poor seagulls without hands –
who went and juggled with the breeze.

'Let's not go home until the waves
stop for the night, daddy.'
                                        The shore
was easy walking, years before.
You may reject what memory saves.

Yet I would tell you if I could.
I only know the way I've gone.
It's not the way to set you on.
Hindsight may show you where I stood.

The waves edge up grubby white paws,
and belly-crawl the pebble fringe,
a scolded mongrel in a cringe.
Scutter of stones and shuffling claws.

Snap

A grandfather speaks

Your mother's eyes, but why a photograph –
stalled mirror that returns the freeze frame,
look, where you'll be, and never be, the same;
in a few weeks the moment's epitaph?

Oh, go on. Fix them the insip. . .ient laugh.
But I shall see from what good mind it came,
this baffled kitten look in your true name –
Girl, twentieth cent. in style, the latter half –

a few years yet but fear what you shall find
beside your mirror every once in a while.
Try not to measure from its poster smile
your secret self glossed in this left-behind.

Others enough will do that for you, mind,
thinking the time of your life is passed in style,
and that a narrow miss is good as her dial.
You grin. Now this long view's another bind.

And what further shall I pluck from the air,
my girl, to guide you through the labyrinth?
The beauty of asphodel and hyacinth?
Their beauty is an annual affair.

Impersonal perfection, specian flair.
We are no figures for a marble plinth,
no columnar rectitude of Corinth,
nor Zeno's specious arrows off nowhere.

It's more like raindrops down a dirty pane,
an inching, gliding to some hindering speck;
some passing confluence that speeds the trek;
then divagations through some crack or stain;

one splitting light, one sloping off in vain,
oddballs that trickle out their little beck.
No child to watch or race them neck and neck,
changing allegiance as they slow or gain.

True gifts of love are transitory: flowers,
wine, food – cash, we both know. Gems, strass, gold, brass,
snaps are the ploys to take possession – pass
the future into memory for hours.

So breathe these words of mine like scents of showers
sprinkled a moment over down-land grass.
– Tears, I've watched tears like raindrops down the glass.
Oh, never come upon these visual powers.

Wishful

FOR KIM

The walks we shared.
Remember that view:
mossed, dry-stone walls
like veins in kail.
How far we saw
from our high hill.

You are grown now
and moved away
into your own life
as you wanted to
and I hoped for you
in your own good time.

I say to myself,
though you're miles off
and I can't see your way
as I used to do,
I'll watch over you
most of the time.

That's what I told you
whenever you needed
but hardly the times
I tell myself now,
and both of us know
it can't really be true.

Still, sometimes I'll think
to watch over you
from a safe distance
for both of us now
whatever we know.
Just imagine it.

Green Brocade

Green brocade of the pre-war table-cloth,
two of my fingers trying to march a line,
stepping in shorn-pile patterns like a path
of puddles strung along the summer lane,

the voice of a slow song, not understood
before forgotten, like water surfacing
under the sill of consciousness, calm mood
of alto sorrow – low, sleepless cradle-song.

To your little soldier, hands up, holding the skein,
you crooned more tears than ever could be yours.
Under my day your wordless voice keens on;
more constant than love, it seeps into the years.

Pavilion

High summer now,
and down a chestnut avenue
they cannot see
dwindling to my vanishing point,
children's voices
shouting in the street maroon me
in that self-blank eternity
when, under the pavilion clock
in its turret,
timing but timed by half-hour trains,
I watched as the gangling shadows
hammed our actions
and worried why.

Railing-clickers,
lights came on in carriage windows
and I was half glad
it was time to go in.

The cries have dispersed to isolations,
like wounded voices on the battlefield,
and the last light has fallen to silence.

Poste Restante

A day like hope.
The sun warms the tulip buds
to open up in the vase on the table,
goblets of light;

your married daughter utters
a turn of phrase that was your wife's,
and it seems
that it would take only a letter
to change, to redeem the past.
The writing starts in your head,
as good as sent.

The patch of sun
has moved from the table top,
an envelope
comes back to you, a strange one,
marked in a scrawl:
'Not known at this address.'

Write 'deceased' across it.
Put it back in the box.

Soliloquy of an Elderly Child-Minder

FOR ELEANOR AND OWEN

I'll not be with you over long.
You won't have come into your own,
the common ground beneath us flown,
except for snapshots, sheets of flong.

Why bother you with so much stuff?
Sorry. Must be that dotty stage
when white hair does for being sage.
I know my onions, all that guff.

Old men, you bet, will garrulate,
spieling some know-how for a whelp
like you to lap up as self-help.
Not me. Best take experience straight.

Most wamble. Who knows where you'll be?
But, if one dusk you're at the lake,
that hush, the storm about to break,
if you were me you'd look to see:

rain-hammered pewter, the lake stops;
spots rivet it against the pane.
An instant rivered off by rain.
Waves for the wind's adzing chops.

You, I know you, rain and your hat,
young Capped-in-Vain. You, too, renowned
for your drenched skirt and your socks drowned.
'Granddad, wake up. What one is that?'

'Stabbing the lawn, the naughty thing?
Woodpecker working his way across.
Look, can you see that patch of moss?
No, no, that flash along his wing.'

. . . The jetty lamp's dust-devil of light.

Copse

Breeze-dappling of leaves
turning on closer sight
to a bunch of sparrows
squabbling in the copse.

It is almost enough.
Three-hundred yards
and thirty years
from where I'd looked.

Tomorrow, sun or shadow,
kids will be here again,
with their high-jinks,
and scatter the sparrows.

The kids will be back
and the sparrows.
And, for the time being,
so shall I.

Cliff-Top

On various benches all along the cliff
rest grey-haired couples – a leg there stiff,
a wrist immobile – watching for their ships
that won't be coming home; the voyages
they won't be making now; clairvoyant clips
into their past that stretches out before
the kids unseen whose yells rise from the shore.

But how tell them? Butterflies, their wings closed,
without apparent motion, yachts repose
across the bay of sunlit frosted glass,
just like, when was it now?, the other day.

Orchard

Not walking by the pathway to the gate,
she swings her leg across the dry-stone wall
where chunks of it have fallen underfoot
of nimble youngsters quick to climb and scrump.
Sunlight through a female blackbird's wings,
the golden brown suffusion of her hair.

And half an hour later she returns,
cradling a bumper crop of plums just picked.
Her skirt is hummocked up two-handed now,
as might be centuries ago to raise from mud
a full-length gown with flounces interlapped
like fringes of the foam as waves withdraw.

And she is happy as the day with plums.
One, half way in her mouth, she dare not bite
for fear with no hand free she loses part
or, going for it, gags on bits of stone.
The taste too good to wait for or to waste.
And now the choice of gateway or the wall.

She looks towards the shortcut, then the plums,
tempted to lift and further bare a thigh.
The equilibrium of the plums decides
and not some notional on-looking gaze.
She backs into the gate, turns, strides away
to winter jams, preserves and homemade wine.

Old notional has eyed leg-shows enough;
the joy of plums is jaded. What he sees
is happiness that's hers or hers or hers,
dwindling like figures in perspective years
back from the dry-stone wall and crop of plums;
skirts lengthening, hair bonneted, furs, skins.

Away Break

Grass grazed to a snooker table baize.
In five collateral beds of long-dry becks
blue velvet shadow.
Kneeling ewes
with legs like charred matchsticks.

It isn't that. Not sheep at all. Those ashtrays
piling up years, odd tick of screwn-up packets,
fag-ends like dead wasps.
Restaurants, bars,
and my serial ahems.

You dying of cancer.
Both of us knowing,
tired old sardonics,
that we can only wish to hope.
'Smoke blows always towards the non-smoker.'

I wish I could recall more of the talk, the jokes.
'Old pastoral throwback,' I can hear you say,
although I never will,
'go back to grass.
Let's get the bill.'

Mottled

Suddenly in mind:
I'd noticed what I thought a rarish bird,
some grouse-like kind,
rich mottled feathers like a Christmas cake,
and had been stirred
to memorize some features of the make,
being bird ignorant,
to tell you as you know the local team
and might identify an immigrant.
But it had been a dream.

Dreams can't be told –
recalled most likely only with some flaw,
lost power to hold.
Today my strange bird had returned to me
because I saw
wet pigeons line a roof, like tiles, to lee
of wind and lashing rain,
a great packed bank of mussels, blue-black.
The journey away from you. The routine train
that won't be taken back.

From long distance here
I'm speaking to you. I beg you do not catch
my words made clear,
like footprints in a night of snow unheard,
a wind-rattled latch,
but out of place and time I give you my word,
broken all other ways,
that when you see wet pigeons now you'll dream
a line in rain that vanishes in haze,
wake to a wordless scream.

Face

If we lived in a different world,
or near enough to try,
I would approach you, girl, and say:
You won't believe my eyes:
yours is the face I've loved for thirty years –
your high forehead,
that urchin-cut,
old half-a-coconut shell.
But I'm not shooting a line.
I know you're someone else.

Somewhere out there's the man I was.
And still I hope you find him –
perhaps you have,
and it may help to know
he has kept faith –
kept faith to thirty years of loss.
– I mightn't know her face these days
if seen by chance.
Nor yet would you,
as like or not.
Goodbye, old girl, go far.

Half-Light

It isn't dark enough, not yet, they think,
to close the curtains on the coming night.

It's dark enough and the air growing chill.
How vulnerable the lights look from outside.

Auburn, the look of her, dressed for a dance
maybe and listening for the phone, his car.

I'm trying not to give another glance.
Lit window thirty years back up that path.

As though time were as pervious as glass
and sight could change the future in the past.

She turns her head. I catch her eye an instant:
grey passer-by she doesn't look at twice.

Curtains are drawn. Mute lights in roomless windows,
like friends I had whose love I walked on by.

Concourse

The women, girls, come to and fro,
some wait and fidget, titivate.
Endearingly unwary moves
I would remember like a scar
if I had been in love – with which?

Leaves on the water through a bridge
on which I lean and contemplate,
with what resistance left, the draw
of roping waters like the claim
of one, who once was lost, returned.

The Walk

Later I christened it 'Thunder Sliver' Walk.
You went along with me and so it became
whenever we'd refer to it in talk
about that year away, a hallowed name.

But, dearest, it was nothing in the sky
nor just an afterthought I'd mused aloud.
A seed pod of the broom had caught my eye,
the one seed-bolted slip of thunder cloud.

I see it now. You had to do it, though,
wangle some common ground. We both do.
The broom I've looked at since that long ago
to find that shade again and show to you.

There. I no longer know if the mind's eye
has kept the colour true as I assume.
We have this pair of words we both hold by.
What took your eye when mine was on the broom?

Skirt

That's it. If you insist:
the flame-coloured full skirt
you wore, years back. We used
to say saffron, for a start.

Saffron: the flaring cloth
I followed miles. You sway
and flag it back and forth.
The very thing, I swear.

Play it for all you're worth.
On your old vermilion bike.
But who are you going with?
You know the way. And back.

Flame, saffron, whatever shades,
but I'm not following blind.
You know where that road leads.
Come back soon from our lost land.

Our Place

I used to cheat in hope.
Time and again I'd take you through the place,
patient as oak,
alert for you to give
some inkling that you sensed it there, if there
it was – some if,
but if we were as one,
the one on good days that we used to think,
response would come.

My mute intuitive,
if you were with me there I would have known.
– No way to speak of it.
The dry valley ascent,
the beeches with their flying-buttress boughs,
and then . . . and then?
– That's where it was in words.
We won't get back beyond them there again;
so have you heard:

an ended peal of bells
whose hum so vies with silence that the mind
hears nothing else.
(These words have done for it.)
Listen. Listen, together now this once.
It won't be missed.
Stop slamming your eyelids.
Listen. . . . That. The silence that's between us.
Hush. Our silence.

Wish

Yesterday I passed that lane,
built up now, but it brought again
your joy at a squirrel's belly-hop
and flop along the chain-
link fence's top.

And I watched a toddler play,
trying to huff the leaves away,
red poncho belling with each hop
stirring the leaves to stray
an inch or two and drop.

Child, so much is beyond our powers.
Leap, leap! And wishing that the flowers
in all the gardens were the same
as in that day of ours,
I gave her your name.

Watching

You'd hear the blanching of the may.
I'm not a tree; there won't be signs.
I outwait you outwatching me.
We've honed it down to pure science.

How you can watch. From dawn to dusk
that lake, remember?, to snap an otter
breaking the stillness of the disc
like a dead man's head in the water.

Watch on. Its skull will be as white
as may. I'll find you it in time.
So keep on. Just you watch and wait.
Stripped clean it will be, quite tame.

That will be easier for you to watch.
Repose it somewhere obvious, safe,
where you can see it as you wish,
another closed book on the shelf.

Intermediary

A flamboyant ghost of may
against the bank of thunder cloud.
You say: 'That blossom phantom's me,
and you're the thunder undeclared.'

Always the need of a third person –
these dumb externals better still –
for us to feed through the old passion.
Come it then, in the high old style.

But may won't serve, nor that dark cliff.
Your turn: 'You have wasted my love.'
Mine next: 'You have wasted my life.'
Now let's get back to make-believe:

Somewhere the thing may materialize,
the third person may ring true,
and one of us may find release
from the bone observatory.

Utterance

When hurt, why do we cry out still?
What utterance ever softened pain,
once staunched the blood-loss from a vein,
once threw the hunters off the kill?

Evolution's treachery
to utilise the weak in death?
(Some creatures' only voice is breath.)
Dear, we must cry more quietly.

Hearth Light

Do the soft darks of winter's hearth
reflect bright noon with its squat shadows?
Your face mysterious in the glimmers,
and darker shadows in your hands,
like small change, copper mixed with silver.
And not a gust has made you turn.

What summer paths that twist and turn,
what shadeless mazes in the hearth,
still gold, will cinder into silver
the forms your memory now shadows?
What warmth is nestling in your hands,
their pulsing blood suffused with glimmers?

I am contented with the glimmers
and not contented, turn by turn.
My life was cradled in your hands;
I burn no memories in the hearth.
Your shades have left me with the shadows.
(All golden sights are glassed on silver.)

And bright noon blackens any silver;
my dazzled eyes prefer the glimmers
that flutter, birdlike, in the shadows,
and, as the birds in spring, return.
Time to heap coal upon the hearth,
lull the suffusion of your hands.

What is there shaping in your hands?
(A darkened pane's like mirror silver.)
Forgotten spirits seek a hearth
but I have only gathered glimmers.
No sudden ghost has made return;
the curtains re-arrange their shadows.

I should remember clearer shadows
like thunderous doves launched from your hands;
the blade of darkness as you turn
your calf; shimmering light of silver
aspen dappling your face with glimmers.
Whose shades are haunting round the hearth?

Shades, love, and shadows round our hearth;
and your cupped hands, suffused with glimmers,
that touch and turn the days of silver.

Pact

Name that I have called upon more times
than any name of God's,
such whispers, blame, so many cries –
hardly murmuring you said:
Some people vow and others vowel.
Blessed are the dead.
– You pleaded with the block I was:
Time. It is time.
Together. Come with me now.
– And inchingly I came.

Look back.
Where is the way we took?
It could end here.
It can't be: come with me.
Not any more.
There is this way,
no other.
Staying is fear;
each step is terror.

Leave me alone.
Break all the words we swore.
I cannot move.
I am afraid that before dark
you will weep cold and pain,
huddled down, face to knees.
And I shall crouch beside you
and when you cry out
from the very bone
begging to die, my hands won't answer you.

TIRADES

TIRADE: Prosody, rare: a passage or speech dealing with one theme.

Eurydice to Orpheus

Down what hole will you dive when I am gone?
What soul song sing to win a look-alike?
'Oh you're so like my rare one when she shone.'?
And which lyre will you play, what poses strike?

And will she dance to grief like love with you?
My, won't you hear me underneath the beat.
I shall be there whatever jig you do.
I shall be getting underneath your feet.

Or will you follow after where I go,
And hope to find the light caught in my hair?
The shadow at my heel points long and low.
I can't imagine what is sung down there.

Sing me a song to make the dark take light.
Can music like a well-rope draw so deep
And not be lost in Lethe and the night
When never once your music entered sleep?

So shall it follow after if I go?
And since I never dreamt it shall I hear?
In such a sleep as that how can I know
The sleep-dance I should do upon the bier?

Your music calmed the animals to stone,
And if your music sounds my sleeping ear
I am afraid I'll turn back into bone.
It takes me all my waking not to hear.

Orpheus to Eurydice

You skitter round till out of breath, you lean
Upon the wall, then through with stone and mortar,
Bird shadow slung across the eye unseen.
Music can't take you like a glass of water.

I never find you still in the green ways
Or in the little towns of cooling stone.
I follow in my music like a maze
But you are off again, away, alone.

Where you have lain my music moves the grass.
And all that follows is your imprint fades.
Where you are still the music breaks like glass.
Your quiet lengthens like the evening shades.

You make me think my music might contain
The muddy gods in warrens underground
And stall the darkness spreading like a stain
Before it stays you like a squirrel's bound.

And when you sleep my music is unstrung.
Your twenty postures, lovely and stone-deaf,
The dreams of statuary tie off my tongue.
The lyric roosts like sparrows on the clef.

Some days I fear that if you were to hear,
Once and for all, the harp would calcify.
And if you die the music in my ear
Would like the swan be mute, and like you fly.

Briefing

I am your future ghost,
    not much before my time.
I'll not be long your guest;
    we shan't much share a tomb,
well, not at least for bed.
    It's your dark shifts I work.
You'll find I'm your best bid
    to outwake your wake.

That means some haunting to do.
    I'll need to plan for effect.
Naked? Via walls or door?
    Clothed? Wounds real or faked?
Further, I'll need to know
    names, addresses, places;
old scores – and pile up new;
    your aims, ploys and policies.

Old soulful myself, so far,
    we haven't met, young bones.
– Sometimes as metaphor
    you admit me within bounds.
(Some say that even God
    was forced to be a man
to crack what flesh and blood
    and good and evil mean.)

That is: I can't assume
    gut-feelings and brain-storms.
Undying love, hate, shame,
    eternal guilt, my terms.
So here are a few good tips.
    You have some time to come,
can take all needful steps
    to plot your little scheme.

A barbed word works a treat.
    But don't aim like a gun;
You fire it on the trot –
    point missed till you are gone.
Yet poignancy stabs better,
    tenderness long lost.
Spent happiness tastes bitter,
    a sweet memorialist.

There's one you must have loved.
    What will you do by her?
Warp up some feeling left?
    Key in a lock of hair?
A turn of hand or phrase
    is usually enough
to make the quick blood freeze:
    the way you hold your knife.

By guilt it is I walk.
    Plant plenty in the living.
If such a ploy won't work,
    nor hatred, fear, last-laughing,
it must be by your guilt.
    I'm sure you can contrive.
– It's much more difficult,
    to stir things from the grave.

Try harder on some friend,
    poor sod, you could betray.
Don't tell me you've refrained.
    A few remain to try.
And if you make your fault
    appear to them as theirs,
your own guilt can be felt
    in double strength for years.

Last, consider your place.
    The haunted also die.
(Grant them a guilty release.)
    Then I'd have had my day.
You must avoid that risk.
    Vital to corner a spot:
path, church, pub, bench or desk
    and let my aura sport.

The after-comers there
    must shudder with some gust,
frequencies in the ear,
    forebodings dimly guessed.
An ancient pile's a plus
    unless some banshee has it.
A headstone's not the place:
    the living never visit.

I am your future ghost,
    come in a nick of time.
Why must you look aghast?
    You are reaching your term.
Few lovers, friends, remain.
    Time to co-ordinate
spirit and canny man.
    Good evening. And good night.

Oh, you remember her,
    the mother and little boy,
begging: that wisp of hair,
    slight build? You passed her by.
Like your Mary she was.
    Remember? Try to react.
That should be good guilt-wise.
    But the spot's overbooked.

Powers of a Tourney

One day you will know
the words I wrote to you
but then, as I always knew,
it will be too late
and I too long ago
for much, love or hate.

You think it's easy to die
and leave the words to you,
words that my life went through,
to you with half an ear
to read and set them by?
Unpenned, the dead appear.

And the ghost writes in stone.
Did you think I'd conform
to type, no longer warm,
that ghosts that breeze through brick
shape easy off the bone?
My white sheets do the trick?

Stray gestures you'd recall,
carefully place – marmoreal,
nothing incorporeal.
This gesture, that? I've scores
you never noticed at all.
They'll shuffle into yours.

Perhaps a bit more cryptic,
dot-and-dah tread, scuff mark.
You'll not be in the dark.
I'll ring your stone-deaf head,
My inner light in triptych
will break like stained glass – red.

Outlook

A woman speaks

What? Gardens, no, not us. Nor the wildlife.
Hasn't been used for years, but there it is.
I thought it might as well look out as in,
not that it sees much now. James had the eye.
We leave it there. His special one it was.
A while back now. We call it James's place.
A good one when we bought it, top of the range.
Beyond us even then. He thought it just the job.
They're smarter now, I know, computerized,
or is it digital? That sunset, cloud.
He took some good ones when he started out.
That great wide weir of light, a level mile,
he said. I never saw so silver-white
a sunset falling on so still a sea.
Like lead, that sea, though, brooding up some grief.
Cornwall, that was, north coast, and summer time,

if I recall, before he went all modernist.
Now he's not here, we don't put those out much,
No, never used it. He was the only one.
He would've shown us how to. But it's his.
His way to see the world, his point of view.
Wouldn't feel right for us to intervene.
Probably useless now, if you ask me,
outmoded. Still uses film. Not how they shoot,
is it, these days, with all this video?
Yes, if we hang on to it, one of these days
it might be reckoned an antique and make
a tidy sum. But it's not going that road.
It's staying put. We call it James's place . . .
and always leave it gazing out like that.
Just about cope, he'd say, with your odd snap.
We've got a simple one for what we take.
A motor-cycle accident. The bike
he reckoned best to get around the place
and . . . scoop his shots up. Quickest at the game.
What was he haring after on that drive?
We'll never know. He'd just say scoop and gone.
The film was blank. Odd it survived the crash,
the camera, I mean. The days I scanned
the papers. Never saw a likely shot.
It's clutter really, but we like it there.
Not much for it to photograph round us.
I peek in the view-finder when I dust.
I like the sight kept clean, no smears or hairs.
It's probably not focused. – That? Wisteria. –
But if you want to take a look through it,
or have a picture? Spares, these. Take your pick.
It's James's place and has been all these years.

Short Story

CHANNEL ISLANDS, 1940–45 – 50TH ANNIVERSARY OF LIBERATION DAY

The Prince's helicopter roared above,
a great liner had anchored near the bay.
Along the front the crowds played push and shove
to see the events of Liberation Day
timed by the shadow on the dial-cum-seat
around the gnomon column. We inched our way
and sauntered off away from noise and heat,
strolled through the bluebell glade to cooler air
along the cliffs and found a bench retreat;
argued what German tourists were doing there,
Then counted reefs with help of surf and spray
and nicknamed yachters in their smugglers' lair
as they played hard at getting under way.
– The worst of shipping waters, so it's said. –
But now it seemed a perfect summer day.
The dazzle of the noonday sun was spread
across the calmest sea like powdered glass.
So intermittently we watched or read.
The liner lowered a launch. The rich first class
embarked to exercise their privilege,
and much as planned, it seemed, things came to pass,
until we noticed someone at the cliff edge
to left of us was standing rapt at gaze.
Sea, rocks below, his eye seemed first to dredge,
and then he fixed his look on the displays
along the front, immobile, unaware
of time or sound, ourselves or the sun's blaze.
So we who felt we had no presence there
ignored his stilled existence, let him peer.
Hard to observe from sun-to-surface glare,
he was, it seemed, in muddy gardening gear
and from his right hand bulged a plastic bag

from Creasey's as if he were a local here.
Not once did his attention shift or flag.
He gazed and gazed in passive truculence,
querulous patience, rugged as a crag.
I shot those glances given when you sense
a face you'd known years earlier might emerge
from features scrawled with time's indifference.
Then, as if driven slowly by some urge,
the figure turned towards us in extreme
perturbation on that thin grass verge
and said, 'Only the dead may safely scream.'
His eye, unwavering, was fixed on me,
the voice too quiet for so harsh a theme.
Then he was gone through dazzle on the sea.
But, as I looked away, at rocks below,
I said: 'My father, killed in forty-three.
– The old face he never was to know.'

Encounter

Where are your followers?
Hell is wide, my lord,
even for harrowers;
dark as the Garden lay
with your cries ignored:
'Take this cup away.'

Take, lord, this cup from me.
Here's the wine-dipped bread,
sodden with treachery:
yours against my soul;
yours against my head.
Share our communal bowl.

You whom I offer this
have betrayed my soul.
Right since the genesis
of created time,
this had been your goal.
Eat your eternal crime.

Week-ending savourer,
you whom I called lord,
I was no waverer,
gave you chance to rise,
rout the Roman horde,
triumph in palms and eyes.

Hung with this lariat,
driven to my grave,
Judas Iscariot,
why me the only man
you set out not to save,
linchpin of your plan?

Week-ending sepulchrist,
what a sacrifice,
for an eternalist,
your three-day spree of death.
A man paid the price.
Oh, save your second breath.

Look, I am turning my
cheek. Kiss it. Rise.

DA CAPO

> 'Da capo, music, to be repeated (in whole or part) from the beginning. [C18: from Italian, literally: from the head]' – adapted from The Collins English Dictionary. The two 'voices' in this sequence alternate, the male speaking first – and then DC.

Return

I have come thirty years back
to watch for you in your old place,
as if I'd recognize your face,
as if your hair were still as black.
Not for that parish con, first love,
but wondering what sort of fist
you've made of things, and if both missed
what once had promised, hand in glove.

The story doesn't change for most,
except for in the pace things go,
and when the realizations show
that all the living haunt some ghost.
A stranger now to strangers, outside
the church where once you went, I wait
in hope to glimpse you at the gate
giving a start you cannot hide.

Ah, is the old curl-flick still a pique?
Your buoyant image clarifies
among the faces. They're your eyes.
Eyes never change. It's time to speak. –
As tongue-tied now as first I was
when all might yet have been. Dead love,
we've no shared past we can relive.
And to the last we go our ways.

Interrogation

Did you come here to sit, or just to yack?
What's so unurgent that you have to tell?
And if to sit, why bother me as well?
But still, I'm glad you've since acquired the knack.

I stay until the last green leaf turns black
on the wild cherry against that sheer cliff
of light. – I'm looking upside-down – as if.
You know my way; the old familiar track.

Why did you think it worthwhile coming back,
after the two-way silence of the years?
Big bangs, is it? Resurrection of old dears,
wobblers in gravity, white holes and black?

No big words now. It's too late, a blue moon.
Blanks, please. Are yours much longer than mine?

Voice Over

Well, I have come back.
There's nothing much to say.
Settled? Let's not speak.
It wasn't an odyssey.

You couldn't divine my way.
I've no clue to your life.
We split; no how or why,
no purchase on old love.

But we've bent the years back.
This is where we began.
Let's sit it out. Don't speak.
How it's all overgrown.

You tried to gather in,
I seem to remember once,
a leaf of every green,
oak, ash, sorrel, quince.

Hundreds of English grasses.
Tints enough for you,
the sedges, reeds and rushes? . . .
My leaves all folio.

The spinney shadows, taller,
close faster than before;
the leaves are losing colour
to take another fire.

Soon we must go away.
How broken is our old oath,
sworn with all reason why,
to put the earth between us.

Recapitulation

You turn at the same angle to the light.
You always did, as if to catch some gist
that lay behind the earth and sky of sight.
You know beyond the hill it's valley mist;
no more to your liking than these leaves.
I have not seen beyond them. Nor have you.

You bore with them awhile, and old Greensleeves,
as I with you. So that's what we shall do.

Questions we could not ask at the right point
spring readily to mind, but it's too late.
I want to guess your life was scant success,
that little planned went right – all out of joint.
I'd like to think you'd tell it to me straight;
but wait to hear a tale made to impress.

Response

You and your leafage. One of the few bits
you managed of the world you meant to save.
But what we pulled apart to be and wish,
how much has weathered all and stands as straight?

But I suppose anyone our age would do
to tally off the hindsight of time past.
Yet we know where we started, what assumed,
and everything that came within our grasp.

The words we swore! Prodigal absolutes.
But it's telepathy we might need now.
I think we'd never know how well it worked
because what came across would match in mood
and thought what emanated.
I went . . . and found
a reed shaken by the wind. It was no search.

Sotto Voce

Where I would return to now is gone.
Where I am I never meant to gain.

Years out, old local maps, like the Holy Book,
have kept a kind of credence looking back.

Once my fingers reached to touch your face.
They cannot clench up thirty years for us,

if that is something either one would want.
Who can be sure how good the way things went?

There is a stillness here and I am still.
There is a time and place where things must stall.

The beasts that fought their corner in a hole
have shaken down in bones their wavering howl.

Where I shall be shall never move from here.
– You couldn't spare an hour the way things were?

Love is the labour we shall not complete.
Watch for the last green in the backing light.

Stop Over

This is no return.
And I'm far off the place,
far away and torn.

I'm not drifting close
to you, this sleepy town.
It took years for release.

It's no triumphal entry;
no prodigal come back;
no retake of the country.

I don't bring much: a book
of hours – years; no bounty,
and no undying ache.

It is the years I am at.
Perhaps you wanted flowers,
rarities, pieces of eight.

It is a wreath: layers
of green not gathered yet
amid that hoard of yours.

Or maybe it will match
something already there.
Perhaps I hoped as much.

The Last Word

Just you remember the wild cherry,
stranger, this grey cloud piling.

With it, I've harried the darkness,
fixing its last green particle.

Now it will hold in your mind's eye,
proof against you and your hindsight,

skulk where you will, my dead ringer
tolling the hours that were steadfast.

Hour

No words. I'll watch with you an hour,
old crosspatch, under the grey tower.

Imagine: there's this afternoon,
a hint of blue shown through the moon,

rough-hewn stone and the rough-hewn cloud.
Rough-hewn. Nothing to say out loud.

Holding hands to cross the road
like kids, perhaps, would be the code.

No roads. All that we have to do
is stay and gaze out on the view.

Encroachments mark for you what's been.
– Am I taken in by the old scene?

It seems enough remains unspoiled –
but the mind's eye is easily foiled.

The valley frays its wraiths of haze.
Enough remains. No past to raze.

– Enough remains. A rough-hewn date;
the rough-hewn years. It's getting late.

So little lies within our power,
old crosspatch, under the grey tower.

Little Enough

Well, love's little enough,
but stauncher than in youth.

Don't bear down over me,
I'm no queen of the may.

If you had stayed around
things mightn't be so ruined.

By heart and rote one learns
the laughter between the lines;

the tenderness behind
the gnarling of the hand.

Stranger, your face is mute.
Lost friend, we've never met.

Gone, if he ever lived,
the young man I once loved.

Ghosts haunt the living past
to change it for their peace.

It will not do, young wraith,
with or without your wreath.

Envoy

Fare well, old love, old innocence.
We hadn't much going for us,
except the inexperience.

The guilt, too, was ingenuous.
It happens to anyone.
We never were synonymous.

But we gave it a good run.
There's nothing more to be said.
It was all a bit homespun.

But now I hear that you are dead,
I look out this dog-eared snap:
you with that tilt of the head.

And after that lifelong gap
I'm thinking again of you.
It's only a bit, a scrap,

but it happens to only a few.
And, though it isn't much now,
it's something you make me do.

I'll leave the picture out.

LENA LATIMER

1939–1992

I HAVE TENDED
ALL THAT I CAN.
BLEST TO HAVE ENDED
WHERE I BEGAN.

Misencounter

This was to be the first and last betrayal,
oh black chrysanth of tousled hair –
not that you'd have picked up any traces.

Still cherished image, once cherished head,
I'm stranded at the window, on the stair.
You looked back once and made your lasting exit.

But I'd have come to this much lower step
to see how years had launched into your likeness,
one glance, stone-calm – to salt away the stealth –

that might have shaken me with time's offence
against the eye of memory. You were to strike me
with a wrench of feeling and affection

for the loving face I live with, frank
with laughter lines and darks not years' alone.
Still cherished head I would have carved in granite,

you'd say, if you could speak from your odd angle,
how briefly memory becomes tall stone.
This is my wreath, propitiatory late white chrysanths.

Not Another Dedication

IN MEMORIAM IAN HAMILTON

Once more, to end as we began
the vicious circle known as life,
in dedication this last leaf
and rhyme enough for you to pan.

'. . . the imaginable moral power',
you once wrote, 'of perfect speech'.
You set your lines to reach that pitch,
the long perspectives, not the hour.

Your voice against oblivion.
– You'd always take the longest odds:
you've made me weep – reading your words.
The times I'd meant to tell you, Ian.

Something ingrained in our war-child years:
tears were the thing to fight against
when drained of every other strength.
And now these words instead of tears.

4

Foursquare

Dedication

FOR N. MURRAY

My mother cautioned me to have no truck
with somebody she called old Nick.
But meeting you was rather splendid luck:
the books you publish are not thick.

The Epigram

The epigram's a blade of light,
    a shaft through storm-cloud, flash
of a secluded pool, this bright
    flick-knife, the headlights' clash,

the teeth of laughter, a smile's sleight,
    lightning, shimmer of dream
across the old familiar night,
    a knot-hole's moted beam,

the shiny elbow of commonsense,
    gloss of the ominous rook.
It comes and goes like truth – and hence
    the darting of this book.

Smashed jars refract along a wall;
the gold nib glitters with the scrawl.

Summary

His nib's
squibs;
the pen's
lens.

A Blade of Light

Waking Thought

We think we love life, hate death,
so why at light's first peep
sigh with the first waking breath
for longer sleep?

Reflection

    Let there be light.
The punishment of Hell is life infernal
And the reward of heaven life eternal.
The joy of living on the earth's diurnal.
    And so good night.

Key to All

Years end up like a clutter-box
of muddled keys to missing locks.

Englishman

This man has double-glazed his leaded windows
to hush Much Havering on the World's loud locals.
In glasses double-glazed his double-gin goes,
and double-glazed his clocks and vari-focals.

Thanks

Such as it is, I love the world through her;
before she came the days were gaps in sleep,
but now they bridge light like a squirrel's leap;
like a sparrow in the hedge, our nights stir.

Secluded Pool

Echo Sounder

Your name
I've called too many times
across a cluttered street
at one face in the rush
too much like yours.

Déjà Vu

The image of your grandmother you seem,
as she recaptured all her ancient dead,
hunching in comfort, cushions at her head.
And I'm the dead you dream.

Walk

Summer. I strolled into a country church
    and sat down, to savour the cool, still air.
Cold-calling, I was left there in the lurch.
    Defunct the intercom; they called it prayer.

Love

If this were not, there would be time
for love to come, and in the prime.
And there was time and time again.
Love, was it then, or then, or then?

Walk

It's a long road.
What I need
is a trickle of silver birch
at the dark turn.

Occasion

If we knew quite when,
dearest, we'd mark the day
unnoticed, that love went;
we'd recognise the date.
Nothing too grandiose:
that walk, say, to the oak.

The Answer

Like any cat curled on a sun-baked wall
you'd only hear your own name
if it suited you playing tame.
Why, being dead, come now at every call?

Leap

Red squirrel carved in wood,
head at the angle that I love.
Let it be one focus. Look,
leaping from my hands to yours.
'Carved wood not tree to tree.'
– Branch to branch, my hands say.

Haunts

D'you think we'd risk the walk along the lake?
It's nothing to us now: no loving look,
no line on staying friends – my hand in yours,
the joy of beating all that space of years.

Flick-Knife

Parents' Evening

Some there are that should not marry;
more there are that should not breed.
Best for the child that she miscarry;
better for him the barren seed.

Slim Volume

New books of verse are like the cat's new litter.
The author has to scrounge good homes for it.
Most must be given away to any victualler.
Who'll put up with and feed poor kit.

Complaint

Poet he styles himself. Like a dead saint,
he leaves us all these relics, sheaf on sheaf.
He ought to stretch to one more fine complaint
upon the rack for his purblind belief.

Flag Day of Fools

Tweed beard sports a golden crucifix;
baldy, a kid's cine badge of tin . . .
It's hard to kick against the pricks.
Dear mother, take me in.

Greaves

Whose name I have not vainly taken
for those who would not do is dead,
these nine years past. By this I'm shaken
but more by how his progeny spread.

Under the Sun

I've seen that pose, and that.
And that one's much too pat.
Try something new instead:
try dropping down dead.

Decorum

Now she whose dainty nipples press-
studded her bikini to her tits –
the only creasing was her slit's –
decorously tucks her knees beneath her dress.

Renascence

Confucius, Plato, Christ, Montaigne and Berkeley,
Blake, Bentham, Mill – he read with sense and system;
he never vainly looked through a glass darkly.
A screwed-up broadsheet bunked his width of wisdom.

Man about Town

The tedium of parties: more booze in the fridge,
more birds in the bed. – He found it anathematory
and in despair he jumped from Clifton Bridge,
gate-crashed the packed all-nighter in the cemetery.

Elsie

Madam, I know we have to share this coach
but I really do not care for your approach.
The brochure offers us sightseeing tours.
No mention there of you sight-saying bores.

Life

It wasn't like it's always going to be.
And this is it as far as I can see.

Bard

So spoke the missionary bard:
I write for people, not the shelf.
– As though a thousand fools' regard
improved a poem silly as himself.

Application

He knew that he had taught them, oh, so well:
concentration, concentration, concentration.
So when it came to his invigilation
they could ignore him, stone-dead where he fell.

Dr Foster

With his discovery of the happy pill
good Dr Foster's cured the most morose.
They say it's just the thing for every ill,
so I have taken a suicidal dose.

The Teeth of Laughter

On Receipt of a Book

Thanks for your most substantial book,
old friend; I read it, line by line,
between two cups of tea, a look
that found some poetry – mine.

Mr Bray

Our Mr Bray agrees with all he addresses,
no matter what the view or predilection.
And in his rear-view mirror acquiesces
with deepest admiration for his full reflection.

Holy Ground

The Reverend Carrick lies beneath this stone.
He used to lie bolt upright too.
And long, I pray, God rest his skin and bone;
he lies at length both straight and true.

The Old Line

'Yes, sir, all steam – and staff all volunteers,
and every one of them worth their salt:
Preservation Society for fifty years.
From Con Junction now to Cripple Halt.'

After-Life

All those believing in the after-life
could not have noticed this one – and his wife.

Retrospective

It was so awful in the past
Why would one want to ever-last?

Poetic Immortality

A life-long atheist, just once, unaided,
I'd like to visit Paradise
to see if rancorous Dante made it.
But what a fool to go there twice.

Aperçu

Few critics label Pound's as verse that tinkles
but as for thought you have to say he thinkles.

Ornithological Discovery

I've discovered why birds sing
what seems for hours before the dawn.
They're counting blossom, trillioning.
Pray God, it soon lies on the lawn.

Ornithological Enquiry

Do birds enjoy a gust shaking the trees?
Is it a free ride, a lullaby by night,
or does it strain their spriggy legs and knees
and give their tiny minds a fright?

Exorcising the Dog from the Guest Room

Dog, scratchy dog, no spirit of Anubis,
give over this absurd, eternal hubris.
Leave in lasting peace these ancient stones.
Go, as in life, and bury your old bones.

'Where two or three are gathered . . .'

MATTHEW 18.20

In youth I gave religion up for dead,
and congregations of two or three.
I took to verse, and poems then read
to audiences of you and me.

The Trinity

Some minds have found the Holy Trinity
an item of profound sublimity.
but three in one suggests lubricity.
I much prefer mankind's duplicity.

Audiences

The pastor preaches to the congregation,
but when he prays he prays surely to God.
They eavesdrop on a private conversation.
The poet speaks to someone just as odd.

Trust

You have deceived me day after day
in idleness and petulance.
But never fear; I won't betray
your ignorance.

A Bad Day Translating French

No one could teach me how to swim.
I take it dry, my pinch of salt.
And bottled water tastes so grim.
I only drink a single malt.
I Englished this rhetorical flannel
to save the Brits crossing the Channel.

Source Texts

I've done three atheists and god.
    Dante was the latter bod.
As for the other chaps
    They did like a good lapse.

On Book-Ends

Between a fickle pair intrude their fool creator,
on shelving overhanging Etna's crater.
Then force-feed him in full the works of ______
until he leans on one and tilts off in his snooze.

A Smile's Sleight

Autumn

That time of year the step has often erred
on what's crushed leaves and what squashed turd.

What Would You Like?

Asked for requests for Christmas, birthday gifts,
I put my closest friends to awful shifts.
They cannot wrap it, pack it, box it, can it,
since what I always want's another planet.

Celebration

Things, wines, we saved to celebrate
those special moments in our lives.
How much longer shall we wait?
The best cutlery has the sharpest knives.

On His Photo in Cycling Kit in the Dale Issue of Agenda

A writer's shins one seldom sees
in photographs of genius
but features posed, magnanimous:
here, in all honesty, the b_____'s knees.

Gloom

I'm filled with gloom. CAUTION: this serial gloom
is packaged not by volume but by weight.
If settling leaves at the top a bit of room,
it is to hell the contents gravitate.

Ostensive Method

Proud father, holding up his toddler,
points skyward to some delta-winger
and says: 'Plane, plane.' Son of aero-modeller
answers, 'Finger, finger.'

Tourism

Stuff Palace, double-deckers, hackney cabs,
rock, candy-floss and ice-cream stalls.
Hushed by the rush of Dochert Falls,
I've seen the burial ground of the MacNabs.

Old Gent's Troubled Night

It's not the drink nor age nor dreams of Hell
that gets me up but the rain hissing.
And it's pouring down so hard I'll never tell
if I've stopped pissing.

Heaven

And when and if I reach the afterlife
and see before me in the celestial buff
the welcome figure of my earthy wife,
which'll say: 'Good God, haven't you had enough?'

Overture

The deity gaily asked the devil
whether he fancied a little revel.
    The devil answered the divine:
    'Fair-dos, I'm game. Your place or mine?'

Curmudgeon

There is a problem with life after death
that, even if a ghost can catch a breath
and shamble back on some nocturnal jaunt,
there's not a place on earth I'd want to haunt.

Concourse Discourse

Thousands of people that I know,
and I'm sitting in a famous place.
I'll wait here in the to and fro
until I recognise a face.

Muse

Words
like birds
come
for some.

On Mirrors, Windows

The best disposed had found it hard to read
until a good spirit gave them the true key,
and rendered crucial help, as they'd concede.
The poem deals with 'Dad, Junior, and Spooky'.

Articulate Bard Interviewed

'Well, poetry's helped me a great deal.
If I'd not put my feelings into verse
they might have come to life, and worse,
I might have sounded real.'

Wisdom

The crucial lesson for a happy life
(not one that I have learnt from my dear wife.)
is this: when any woman says it's hot,
or cold, agree – weather it is or not.

Rhyme and Reason

My dear old fellow poet Michael,
how odd that you should rhyme with cycle.
    But if I call you Mike,
    You still must rhyme with bike.

Shimmer of Dream

Secrets

She used to murmur in unguarded sleep
the loving pet-names in her Norman Conquest
but now they man the everlasting keep
she snorts three different snores that lasted longest.

Insomnia

Silence, heartbeat, bustling breath.
Sleep? No brother let it be to death:
even on the darkest night
the window lets in too much light.

Love Talk in Age

No wish to join the garrulous old bores,
but could you tell, between you and your snores,
this gurgle as of pipes, this creak of floors,
is it my stomach, or one of yours?

Obit

Everything he ever did;
every inch he would not give,
part of a single-minded bid
to write some poems that might live.
A chronic case requiring medication
known in the métier as *ded*ication.

The Old Familiar

Upmanship

You promise yourself to recognize them first,
features unblurred by time, or not too much.
Mortified to catch that phrasing long rehearsed:
'Old friend, how come we drifted out of touch?'

Forty Years On

So much of life's a long drift trying to place
a half-remembered look, once loved, once proud,
no chance misrecognition in the crowd.
– And, there, that's surely Bone's familiar face.

Crusader

You sleep more on your back as you get older.
Is it to get an easier breath
or since you can no longer cold shoulder
death?

Journey

The way is dark. No lamp, no window's glow
and I am terrified to run or sidle.
– No one is hiding there. Not far to go.
Just to that corner. Then you can rest bone-idle.

Thesaurus

Poetry's a thesaurus: my pigeon, your dove.
Here are the elegant variants for love;
here are the alternatives to death;
one, on the tip of my tongue, gasping for breath.

Staple Diet

You know you're getting old beyond all doubt
when the box of staples has run out.

Concert

I cannot hear the music, grasp the song.
A stranger's features in the rows ahead
have brought to mind loved faces,
long estranged, or dead.

Omnibus Edition

The days of childhood are the longest,
of youth the most intense,
the middle years first right, then wrongest
and old age is whence.

Like Truth

Echo

Echo loved Narcissus; his self-conceit
reduced her to a second voice
as pale Narcissus made his choice,
self-love, and never would repeat.

Literacy

An old woman, I am taught to read
by this young girl with clear voice and looks.
She puts into my gnarled hands tidy books.
She doesn't have the words I need.

Restraint

In time-tried English custom the orchestral
conductor's one of few that are allowed
public emotion. – Calm your stress cholesterol.
He has to keep his back toward the crowd.

Philosophy

Two great evils none can quell:
not being able to stand yourself.
But worse for everybody's health:
standing yourself too well.

The Truest Art

Poetry is the fiend that lies like truth
and tells such whoppers in our giddy youth
but with the coming of uncertain age
its white lies shoot a line in shades of beige.

Dying

Dying's like going to the lavatory;
it's best to do it on your own.
More so if it's all cathetery
or you want to grunt and groan.

On Guildford Cathedral

I raised a brick to bring this hope to pass
(that was, admittedly, in my mad youth).
Now its uncluttered lines and crystal glass
are stained by richer men and lesser truth.

Thought in Passing

I cannot stand the Vatican and popery.
I can't abide the protestant pot-pourri.

With the Gift of a Book

I've sent this book, my once and future friend,
not that you'll read it. No change there, I trust,
but so that someone latches on it in the end
up in your attic, like a splinter in the dust.

Friendship

What good is it for me to say:
I never varied in our friendship, not a day
in all the years we were apart?
In all the years we were apart.

Prescience

'Let there be enzyme soup,'
God said; 'I'll watch it group
itself into a mind
that learns it's not designed.
And once it's thought up souls,
I'll let it find black holes.'

The Shiny Elbow

Ups and Downs

However slight the rise is to the crown
a cyclist going up the hill
detests the cyclist coasting down
then gloats on those who're climbing still.

Lines for a Putative Grandson

Son of my son, I wish that in your youth
he'll be as reasonable as I would be,
and you, as stubborn and uncouth
as he to me.

Experience

Young toughs tattoo themselves to look much braver
but do the puny rest of us this favour
when, later on, their tattooed arms remind
us how youth's follies are not left behind.

Guest

Ah, you've been long expected, pain in the chest.
The tedium of wondering whether you'd arrive.
But now you muscle in as a house guest
don't park your write-off on my drive.

Boxing and Coxing

My father's aching bones his lame excuse,
I thought, to shorten horse-play games with me.
Now his age, nor a shade the more obtuse,
I feel this bone-ache in Monopoly.

The Wealth of Experience

Few things – not Hitler – raise such hate,
such blinding rages in the soul
as does the umpteenth toilet roll
that will not tear its sheets off straight.

Middle-Age

My childhood was too hot, old age too cold.
There was a fortnight, neither young nor old,
that was just right.
but I was tight.

Missing

The ‘borrowed’ gaps on shelves,
slight poet, slant essayist.
Good God, their words more missed
than absent friends themselves.

Political Engagement in the Arts

A man with fire in his belly
to right the world’s wrong
would break into the telly,
not into song.

Upbringing

We teach frustration from the earliest days
and so develop desiccated man:
the brat pisses his heart out in the pan
but fixed the water level stays.

Civility

Even when furious with the cat
I let her in because she trusts me to,
and I’m flattered by all of that.
With humans, this would never do.

Snap

Old mentors, I've at last forgiven you.
I cannot spare the hatred any more.
Now an old fogey, I've enough to do
hating the callow youth I was before.

Mother's Day

He wears a brooch in mother's praise, the arse-hole.
– Every tyrant had one. Once the jig began
she was the jiffy wrapping of a parcel,
as he is but the wrapping of a man.

Applause

Applaud, applaud, and raise the roof.
The loaded silence must not linger,
for fear the passion of the singer
enter the soul like truth.

Poetaster

A bad poet's still a poet
as a bad man's still a man,
Chesterton wrote, and he should know it.
The works of neither should you scan.
The difference is clear: the crook
not poet should be brought to book.

Father's Advice

Things exposed to the air
are subject to decay.
If you would get some heir
poke the thing away.

Treadmill

Some see it plainly as the point on a knife
but search me if I've got the point of life.
Likewise, I've never seen the point of death.
So here we go again. Don't hold your breath.

The Gold Nib

T. S. Eliot: 1929

If I cannot have kings and such deference,
a nation whose art is to rest on its knees,
I shall settle for cats and your reverence
and rituals of biscuits and cheese.

Grand Old Man of Letters

Folk always say I'm full of gloom
  and telling tales of woe;
but as for that I have the room:
my last friend upped and found a tomb
  these twenty years ago.

Footnote

Larkin, Larkin, you've got it wrong again:
that arrow shower somewhere becoming rain.
Not then, but twenty, thirty years to land
when one is bent giving the other a hand
as both had promised long ago they would
when nothing more could come to any good.

Genius

A genius, his thing was, every night,
to stay up talking for his friends' delight.
His mistress never could conceive the worth
and his name perished from the earth.

Coles Notes to Jane Austen

When it comes to love or money, Sir Bill Fold,
her heroines are good as gold;
all that clitoris is not cold
and comes freehold.

Apology

Sorry, Laforgue, for shaky French,
your wit strained through my Saxon sieve.
Only rapport could have the gall to give
your French épée an English wrench.

Style

Hear Yeats who's not a proper Herbert swear
that all good structure's in a winding stair.

Infamy

He's been neglected far beyond his worth;
his name's anonymous around the earth
which gives his talent, modest and abstemious,
the thundering silence it reserves for genius.

In memoriam: G.O.M.

How curious that when a great bard dies
a thousand mortal pricks at once indite
glum verses full of water-metered sighs
as if his memory lay in what they write.

Ivory Tower

If poetry can't come from normal life
then it isn't worth a light.
Would you mind passing me that knife?
Only madmen live to write.

Post-Gutenberg

Puzzling how every post-modern performance bard
turns out so keen to spill his spiel across the page
while poets of the page feel quite ill-starred
in spouting out their lines on stage.

Maxims

Look in thy heart and write. – A duty
that would require a surgeon's knife.
– Art holds a mirror up to nature's beauty?
– It pisses the shit off the pan of life.

Preface to Dante

Dante had mighty Latin, meagre Italian
but chose his native tongue to weather time.
Neither's my forte; in Shakespeare's saucy galleon
I hoist the triple sail of Dante's rhyme.

Anon

Practitioner of the most private art
in which the greatest have no name,
he mopes around the house or mopes apart
because he hasn't got a ghost of fame.

The Poetry Library

Wrongly replaced on the book shelf,
why is Rimbaud's *A Season in Hell*
next to Walt Whitman's *Song of Myself*?
The difference, though, is hard to tell.

Silent Reading

The bind about the National Poetry Library
  is that the readers – no, don't look –
(from Earl's Court, Samarcand to Highbury)
  intrigue you more than any book.

National Poetry Day

Writing poetry's like keeping bees.
It takes commitment and some expertise.
Bees can't be swapped for butterflies that pack
no sting, no honey, nor swarm to an attack.

Demise of a Poet

'I don't feel happy with abstractions.' So he said.
And when at last he faced the concrete, stone dead,
his soul was not so much put out as quite put down
and he became an immaterial noun.

All Poets are Liars

Every dictum said of verse is right
    with one restriction:
any pair that aren't in contradiction
    aren't worth a light.

Colloquium

'Your early work has not worn well,
its jagged feeling losing power.'
'Ah, what you mean but cannot tell
is that it's young, you old and sour.'

Ominous Rook

Englyn: Peace

If there is peace in the green grave,
better haven than we've seen,
why has no zealous revenant been back
to tell us all and make us keen?

Eulogy

Married twenty years we were.
Late? He was always early.
Poor little mouse-cub without any fur,
too soon for this hard journey.

Retrospection

Poems that bore the weight of truth
when we were young now in our age,
whenever we turn back the page,
are lays that fleeced our misbound youth.

Minimal Accommodation

Well, this will have to be the bedroom
because there's precious little headroom.

Epitaph

Love, love, the dreams were Hell.
Do not ask if I sleep well.

Coming up Trumps

Dying is ghastly but death is all right.
My friends and I enjoy a good night.
    We hate alarm clocks.
    They give us the hump.
    So stuff the Last Trump.
    Here's to *perpetua nox*.

Testamentary

Bung me the cheapest of burials possible.
Drop me in any old dirt that is fossable.
– Written for dance and matters idyllical,
this is a measure considered dactylical.

Column Shorter than Nelson's

Follow no hearse;
intone no verse.
Drop in the earth
not a tear's worth.
Forget the man;
keep what will scan.

Envoy

The trouble with youth is
  you get it all wrong.
We thought the truth is
  something in song.

The trouble with age is
  you get it all wrong.
We thought we were sages
  and lingered too long.

Notes

To Aspen *page* 31

The poem refers to 'The Aspens' by Edward Thomas. In the last line, the Morse Code symbol '. . .' represents the letter S – a serpentine form.

Second Comeback *p.* 37

'But whosoever offend one of these little ones . . . it were better for him that a millstone were hanged about his neck, and that he were drowned in the depth of the sea.' (Matthew 18.5).

Second Reading *p.* 41

The phrase 'gem-like flam' is a reference to Walter Pater's phrase, once fashionable in artistic circles: 'To burn always with this hard, gem-like flame, to maintain this ecstasy, is success in life.' *Studies in the History of the Renaissance.*

Way Out *p.* 42

Eddie Wolfram was a childhood and lifelong friend, a painter.

The Unknown Flower *p.* 46

The title glances off Edward Thomas's poem title 'The Unknown Bird'. His pseudonym as a poet was Edward Eastaway. He lived at Steep.

And There Was Light *p.* 49

'And God said, "Let there be light" and there was light.' Genesis 1.3. During the black-out of the Second World War, my elder brother was allowed out after dark but I was not.

Heugh *p.* 50

W. S. Milne is a Scot; hence the change in language.

Eighth Period *p.* 58

In stanza one, the second line is an ironic parody of Ben Jonson's line 'Queen and huntress, chaste and fair.' *Cynthia's Revels*, 5.iii. Similarly, the bracketed sentence in stanza 3 refers to Shakespeare's line in *Henry V*, 'Once more unto the breach, dear friends.' (4.iii.1). The sentence following is from *Antony and Cleopatra*, 4.xiv.

Obtainable at all Good Herbalists' *p.* 65

This herbalist's, in New Inn Hall Street, Oxford, was well-known among students in the sixties for selling condoms.

Unaddressed Letter *p.* 71

The quotation in stanza two is adapted from Revelation 21.4.

The Fragments *p.* 72

The quotation at the head of the poem is from a book of hymns by Albert Orsborn, *The Secret of his Presence*. He became the General of the Salvation Army, a teetotal organisation, during my childhood. A teenage sense of irony found imagery of a tavern in the quotation.

The quotations after verse one and two are from Shakespeare's *King John*, 3.iv, lines 90, 93.

The last line of stanza 3 refers to John 11.25.

The single line following refers to Matthew 10.39.

The quotations in the next stanza, 4, refer to Philippians 2.5.

The quotation concluding stanza 5 refers to Isaiah 55.1.

Some of these quotations from the Authorized Version have been slightly adapted.

Thinking of Writing a Letter *p.* 78

In stanza four, the quotation from Yeats is from 'Two Songs from a Play', 2.

Full Circle *p.* 83

The novel is *Moonfleet* by J. Meade Falkner. The remarks about senior pupils in stanza three refer to a bad practice of the school whereby classes of absent teachers were divided and distributed to the back rows of other classes, irrespective of age, subject or abilities of themselves or the classes they arrived in.

Music *p.* 117

The last line echoes Wordsworth's 'Solitary Reaper': 'Will no one tell me what she sings?' Presumably she was singing something in Gaelic.

Bird's Eye *p.* 126

'Birsy' in the last line is the imagined corruption of 'bird's eye' on analogy with 'day's eye' which is now 'daisy'.

Compact *p.* 129

The opening line derives from Shakespeare's sonnet 92, line 2.

The Garden Beyond and Beyond *p.* 190

Just after the Second World War, fountain pens were expensive items not thoughtlessly given to children.

Not Another Dedication *p.* 249

The quotation is from Ian Hamilton's biography of Robert Lowell, his remarks on *Life Studies* in chapter 15: 'his one remaining faith, if one can call it that, is in the imaginable moral power of perfect speech.'

Index of Titles